LENGTHENING GOD'S ARM

A Jesuit's Life and Thoughts

JAMES L. CONNOR, S.J.

Apprentice House Press
Loyola University Maryland

First Edition

ISBN: 978-1-62720-307-4

Printed in the United States of America

Cover photo: Portrait head shot of Father Connor taken outside the Woodstock Theological Center at Georgetown University, June 2002.

Cover image: Rev. James L. Connor, S.J., Director, Woodstock Theological Center (1987-2002). Photo, and photo with Rev. Walter J. Burghardt, S.J., courtesy of The Woodstock Theological Library Archives, Georgetown University, Washington, D.C.

Apprentice
House Press
Loyola University Maryland

Apprentice House Press
Loyola University Maryland
4501 N. Charles Street
Baltimore, MD 21210
410.617.5265
www.ApprenticeHouse.com
info@ApprenticeHouse.com

Contents

Part III. Mission: Contemplation and Action, in a Troubled World

Part IV. Leadership: Principles and Practices for Business and Life

Foreword

Father Connor teaches that gratitude is the foundation of all else in Christian life. This book is an occasion for gratitude. Having known Father Connor for 40 years—an appropriate biblical number—I looked forward to his upcoming book. I now have read it and let it seep in, and then repeated the process. There are multiple reasons to welcome this book. Here are three.

First: This book will become your companion, if you allow it. In honoring Father Connor on his 50 years as a Jesuit, Father Walter Burghardt, whose toast is the Afterword of this book, thanked his friend "best of all" for being a Companion of Jesus. As a Companion of Jesus, Father Connor became a companion to all whom he served. This book ensures that his companionship will endure. This book lengthens Father Connor's arm—and thus the arm of Our Father.

Second: Father Connor starts his book with a memoir of his life. The memoir is not only autobiographical; it also teaches. To fit 90 years into approximately 50 pages required Father Connor to select the events that, with the wisdom of hindsight, retain their importance. Those selections contain lessons. God calls, sometimes clearly to a six-year-old boy, sometimes delphically to a young theology professor. Then, at each turn, Father Connor names and thanks those who guided and helped him as he responded to God's call. As Father Connor notes, Saint Ignatius' conversion began by reading about the life of Christ and the saints. Our own little conversions may draw strength from reading this memoir. And remember the gratitude. Each of us will "write" our own memoir—a few on paper, but mostly as we tell our stories over time. If nothing else, come back to thank those who guided and helped us, as the tenth leper did and as Father Connor has done here. For those whom Father Connor taught—directly and through this book—our gratitude will be yet another way to lengthen Father Connor's arm.

Third: The remainder of the book consists of selected reflections on the Scriptures, the challenges facing our world, and leadership. The reflections can be sneaky. They draw you in gently, but if you accept the book's invitation to join in the Ignatian mission, the hard work begins.

Although each reflection stands on its own merits, the reflections also teach us how to proceed. Throughout the book, Father Connor discusses the process of Ignatian discernment, which underlies these reflections. We will have missed one of the book's greatest lessons and gifts if we don't use these reflections to serve as the catalyst for our own reflections on how to discern and respond to God's call in a troubled world.

Father Connor tells us that one of the wisest lessons he learned as a new provincial was to listen. As you take up this book, follow that advice. Don't just read; listen. Listen—with courage, humility, and gratitude.

Nita Crowley is a lay colleague of Father Connor.

Introduction

Father Jim Connor began drafting the autobiographical section of this book several years ago, and the project expanded to include his broader reflections on faith and life.

Part I is the autobiographical portion, on which he worked closely with Beth Kostelac, and in which he writes about multiple turning points in his life. These include his insight—at six years old—that God was calling him to be a priest; a mystical as well as mysterious experience as a young Jesuit at Loyola University of Baltimore (a voice bidding him and other Jesuits to return "home" to their spiritual roots); the upheavals of the 1960s that unexpectedly tossed him into the role of Maryland Jesuit provincial, at age 39; his dramatic first encounter with the beloved Jesuit Superior General Pedro Arrupe ("I knew at that moment that I would walk on burning coals for that man"); and his recent struggles with Alzheimer's ("I tell people these days—semi-seriously—"I don't DO proper nouns anymore!").

Part II is an edited collection of Father Connor's homilies as pastor of Holy Trinity Church in Washington, D.C., culled from three thick binders of sermons he typed out during the early-to-mid 1980s. He ushers us through the liturgical year, with down-to-earth homilies that have retained their freshness. They're presented under titles and subtitles such as "Is this Mary's Boy? Jesus Grows Up Fast," "Jesus the Partygoer: At a Wedding, in Cana," "The Craziness of Pentecost: Giving Away Love, Peace, and Freedom—Free of Charge," and "When Peter and Jesus Had Words: 'You Satan!'"

Parts III and IV—"Mission" and "Leadership," respectively—draw mostly from speeches and other unpublished reflections by Father Connor over the past five decades. He ranges over topics like the nature of Jesuit education (he notes that the product of an enterprise such as business education at Loyola of Maryland "is not a degree, but a person—the person who is the student today and who will be a leader tomorrow"). He writes about people and events including the martyrdom of six Jesuits in El Salvador, recalling his time spent with them at the University of Central America ("What I remember most were the bullet-pocked walls in the living room of their residence. There had been any number of drive-by machine gun shootings"). And he speaks of mission, ministries, and apostolates, often about the Ignatian spiritual apostolate (see Part IV, chapter 36, his three simple questions for capturing the unfolding steps in the Jesuit Examen: "What happened?" "So what?" and "Now what?").

Both of us worked at the Woodstock Theological Center during Father Connor's time there as director, and Beth also worked with him previously at Holy Trinity Church. We are deeply grateful to all those—parishioners, Woodstockers, and others—who gave encouragement and otherwise lent a hand to these efforts.

Finally, we are grateful beyond words to Father Connor. We thank him for an apostolic life devoted to extending the divine reach—lengthening "God's arm" (see Part III, chapter 26, last paragraph)—in our lives and our world.

—Beth Kostelac and William Bole, the Editors

PART I

Life ...

From 1929 to Now

1.

Discerning a Vocation, at Six Years Old

From Birth to High School Graduation, 1929 to 1946

I was born in Philadelphia, Pennsylvania, on May 21, in the Year of Our Lord, 1929, to Martin Francis Connor and Mary Kilpatrick Connor. My father would often say to me in jest, "Two horrible things happened to our family that year: I lost all of my money and you were born!" The Wall Street crash of 1929 ushered in the Great Depression and our immediate family was hit hard in the pocketbook, more so than I realized when I was a small child.

When I was a little older and able to understand, my mother would tell me that I was *conceived* in a very well-to-do family and then, nine months later, I was *born* into an impoverished family. And we really lived that way. The family's prosperous coal/oil company was reduced to one oil truck, parked right in front of our row house and of which my father was the only driver. As a little boy, I'd deliver newspapers, or cut grass on the lawns of our neighbors, to earn a little money. We grew vegetables in what previously had been flower gardens so we'd be sure to have something to eat.

Still, it was a happy childhood. We were knit closely in the Connor family—my parents, my siblings (older brother Marty and younger sister Mary Jane), and my grandparents. Our economic circumstances lent toward our closeness, in a way. Because of our financial setbacks, we had to sell our house in Philadelphia and move into my paternal grandfather's huge house, just a few blocks away.

My grandfather was one of five Connor boys who had started a coal business throughout the city of Philadelphia, and eventually converted

3

it into an oil business. He was assigned to the North Philadelphia sector of this business and did very well professionally and financially. He had recently retired when we moved in with him, so he had a lot of time to spend with a four-year-old youngster like me. He would seat me on his knee and sing barbershop songs like "I want a girl, just like the girl that married dear old Dad." I loved following along with him, and singing has been with me ever since.

I was also very close to my maternal grandfather, James Lester Kilpatrick, who was president of the New York Telephone Company from 1933 to 1941. He too was born in Philadelphia, on July 9, 1876. He had begun his career in the employ of the Bell Telephone Co. of Philadelphia, climbing telephone poles and streaming wires. He never had the schooling that his children and grandchildren would enjoy, but he was very bright and capable, and eventually he made it to the top. He rose through the ranks with that company to become assistant vice-president and general manager. Then, he was appointed vice president of New York Telephone Co. in 1927 before ascending to the presidency. After retiring, he continued with the company as a director until 1949. We would visit him in his Park Avenue penthouse during the Christmas holidays and had great times.

For several years, his Christmas present for me and my brother Marty (older by a little over a year) would be summer camp in New Hampshire. I had never been outside the Philadelphia/North Jersey area, and my introduction to Camp Sunapee was my first time away from my mother and father. Up there in New Hampshire, I had unprecedented freedom to care for myself, to decide things with relative independence, and to express myself so frankly. We took a canoe trip down the Connecticut River over three days. We climbed Mount Washington in two days, spending the night on a rocky slope in sleeping bags. We were free to go to church on Sunday—or not. (When we returned, my mother believed Marty and I had turned into savages.) Camp Sunapee was a blast, with adventures for two or three weeks, and it was all thanks to our grandfather. He was one of my all-time heroes, not just for his role in the family but for the way he devoted himself to work and to the emergence of his talents. James Lester Kilpatrick was a leader. He passed in 1962.

I was named after Grandfather Kilpatrick, which explains my distinguished middle name of "Lester." I remember that all through grade school my middle name was a cause of great consternation for me. The nuns could not understand how my good Catholic parents could have given me that name since there was not a Saint Lester! But that's getting just a little ahead of the story.

As I turned five, I was terribly lonely without my brother, Marty, who had already started school. Over time, in my loneliness I became petulant and unruly at home, so my mother attempted to enroll me in the kindergarten of a public school near our house. But after getting into trouble for fighting with other students, I left the public school. Then, my mother went to see the nuns at our church, Little Flower, and convinced them to take me into the first grade of the parish school—at age five. (Many Catholic schools did not have kindergartens at the time.) Perhaps thinking—incorrectly—that I would be as good a student as Marty (who had leaped ahead to 2nd grade by that point), they let me in, thank God.

We already knew the nuns well. They lived in two houses on the same block as ours, and they would let us cut through the grounds of their residence as a shortcut on the way to grade school. We were also under strict orders from our parents that if the nuns ever came out on their back porch and clapped their hands, we'd better go out and help them, or else. It was, as I said, a happy childhood, in a friendly neighborhood with a wonderful education and supportive parents.

Many people spend years, even decades—in high school, college, or further into adulthood—trying to discern a religious vocation. And they do so rightfully and fruitfully. I arrived at my sense of vocation at six years old. I remember one night lying in bed, staring up at the ceiling and thinking about the catechism we were using in school. It was the legendary "Baltimore Catechism," and the first question was, "Why did God make me?" The correct answer: "God made me to know Him, to love Him, and to serve Him in this life and to be perfectly happy with Him forever in the next." And I thought, "Gee, that's what it's all about. How can I best do that?"

And it occurred to me, "I don't want to spend the rest of my life as a Fuller Brush salesman for goodness sake." For me, a door-to-door salesman epitomized everyday, ordinary business. So, I said to myself, in my six-year-old way, *if knowing, loving, and serving God is really our primary goal in life, I'd better do it as directly as I can.* And from what I had been able to see in our parish church, I thought that being a priest was the best way to do that. A priest can bring people to God and God to the people in Baptism, Mass, Communion, Confession, and Last Rites. In so doing, you are also serving God in the best way possible. Therefore, I thought: *I ought to be and I want to be a priest.*

Afterward, becoming an altar boy only reinforced my decision, since it enabled me to get to know the priests in our parish very well. They would train boys like me to serve at Mass and to assist in baptisms and other sacramental liturgies. I came to know them as priests, but also as the coaches of our parish football, basketball, and baseball teams, which competed with rivals at other Catholic schools in North Philadelphia. Their leadership on the field also made a distinct impression on me, and made the priesthood seem like a very high calling indeed.

Then, it occurred to me, "What if you're not happy as a priest?" "Well," I said to myself, "I'm only going to live until I'm 65." I remember saying "65" because I thought that meant a very old man on the verge of death—though I'm 90 right now! But what I really meant was that even if I were to be miserable for all those years, I would have been doing the right thing. So, I said to myself, "I'm not here in life just to be happy. I'm here in life to be serving others as Jesus did. So, I'll just embrace the risks and do it as well as I can." It was really plain and clear, maybe even simplistic.

Another motivation to the priesthood was that my paternal grandfather had a brother who was a priest. He was my Granduncle Harry, a diocesan priest. He used to take his summer vacation at Beach Haven on the Jersey Shore, where my grandfather had a house. We would stay there too, often when Uncle Harry was there, and both my brother and I always enjoyed our time with him. Uncle Harry died when I was in the third grade. At every parish in the archdiocese, they would make the announcement when one of the priests died. On that Sunday they announced, "Please pray for Father Harry Connor who died this past week," and in the back of my head I heard a voice say, "Don't worry, folks, it won't be long before another Father Connor will come along." I remember these instances really clearly, so that whenever someone asks me, "When did you think of being a priest?" I feel like saying, "I never thought of being and doing anything else. It was the logical thing to do."

Becoming a *Jesuit* priest was a different matter—another discernment, later on. That happened in high school. A little background, first: my brother Marty is sixteen months older and also much brighter than I am. Before he graduated from grade school, he took a scholarship exam at Saint Joseph's Prep, a Jesuit school, and won the scholarship for half tuition. I came stumbling along a year later and took the scholarship exam—and, as usual, won nothing.

My father declared, "I'm not going to have one boy at this fancy school run by the Jesuits and another down the street going to the parochial high school or the public school." It came down to that, because my parents couldn't afford to pay full tuition. So my father went downtown and spoke to the principal, Jesuit Father John Lenny. Driving a hard bargain, he told the priest that unless I got a half-scholarship, my brother would be withdrawn and sent to a public school with me. I'm sure it helped quite a bit that Marty was one of the stars there, from the get-go, in his freshman year. Anyhow, that's how I got to the Prep, and when I arrived there I came to know and admire some of the Jesuits, especially the young scholastics. It was my experiences and relationships at St. Joseph's Prep that made me warmly motivated to become a *Jesuit* priest. Most likely, I would not be a Jesuit if I hadn't attended a Jesuit high school—and if my smarter brother wasn't in such demand at that school!

During my first year at the Prep, I felt "called" to take up a musical instrument because I noticed that Saint Joseph's College had a band that played and marched at their football games. So, eventually I volunteered to join the high school's band, with saxophone as my preferred instrument. During my freshman fall semester, I started traveling to school on Saturday mornings to be taught how to play the saxophone and to learn how it "fit" into a band and an orchestra. Our instructor was a member of the Philadelphia Symphony Orchestra and he taught us a variety of ways the saxophone could be used: from symphony to dance band. My parents rustled up the money to buy me a tenor saxophone and I began using it in our high school band, in a small parish group playing for dances, and later in an ensemble that traveled around to perform. In formal high school concerts, I also played the much larger, bass saxophone. And, at events like school dances, our small group (piano, saxophone, trumpet, and clarinet) would lay aside our instruments and sing as a vocal quartet. While still in high school, I also learned to play the piano using money from summer jobs to take lessons in downtown Philadelphia.

The jobs were a constant in my young life. Entering my teens, I worked in a paint factory one summer. Then, when I was about 15, I got a job on a road crew in Beach Haven, New Jersey, while staying at my grandfather's summer house there. I loaded the cement mixer with cement and sand, and pushed it in a wheelbarrow for the men laying it on the sidewalk and curbs. I think I was making about 50 cents an hour. And then I got a BIG raise—to a dollar an hour—when a 70-year-old man named Pete Lane, who was a mason, hired me to be his "right-hand boy." Pete was as salty as they come, as was his language and worldly philosophy! I helped him lay cement sidewalks, put in stone steps, build brick chimneys, plaster walls, and so on. We sometimes worked with crews—men who had never gone to or graduated from high school. They loved to tease me as a "fancy prep school type." We got to be really good friends, and I was able to earn money that went directly to my parents for our family support.

All that was part of my childhood. I knew poverty—but also simplicity, which could be translated into a life of service to others. The circumstances enhanced my vocational discernment.

My *Jesuit* discernment process went into full swing, reaching a high point when I took part in a retreat for seniors directed by Jesuit Father Louis Wheeler. What permeated his retreat was the sentence, "To know God's will and to do God's will—not counting the cost." He really got me thinking, and near the end of the retreat, I went to see him and asked, naively, what exactly that will was for me, vocationally. He told me that I should go and talk to a Jesuit who knew me. I thanked him and later made an appointment to talk with Father Lenny, the principal at Saint Joe's Prep. When I told him that I was wondering whether God was inviting me to be a Jesuit, he sat back and roared with laughter. "Why in the world would you want to do that?" he asked. But then, when he had settled down, he said, "OK, let me tell you how you might discern and discover whether God is calling you to that or not."

He explained to me the process of Ignatian discernment. "First, sit down some day when you are calm and collected and on a piece of paper write: 'Reasons why I should apply to enter the Society of Jesus.'" And, he said, "Put down every conceivable reason, even those that on the surface seem superficial or silly. Then, on another day, do the same thing, except now the column should be headed with, 'Reasons why I should not apply to enter the Society of Jesus.' Then on a third day take both lists—the pros and the cons—and compare them and go down each list putting a checkmark behind the reasons that seem most influential to you. Finally, on a fourth day, look at the items you have checked and try to discern and decide which ones are most influential and, therefore, are guiding you to a decision."

Then he said, "When you've done this come back and we can talk about it—and try to discern where, in fact, God is leading you." I did so and the rest is personal history. I submitted an application to enter the Jesuit Maryland Province, and was accepted. I was 17 years old.

2.

Digging Graves, Singing *a Cappella*—and the Spiritual Path

In Formation, 1946 to 1960

I entered the Jesuit novitiate, at Wernersville, Pennsylvania, on July 31, 1946. It may sound amazing today, given the shortage of priestly vocations, but I entered the Society of Jesus along with no fewer than 14 of my high school classmates from St. Joe's. One of the first things four of us did upon entering was to form an *a cappella* quartet: Tom Pyne, Buck Spillane, Bill McFadden, and myself. All through the Jesuit course of studies, I sang in the choirs and occasionally was the soloist of particular hymns. My passion for music and singing, instilled at the Prep, served me well in my years of Jesuit formation.

The first two years in the novitiate were devoted to formation in Jesuit spirituality and life. Though we did other things: for example, I was appointed "Senior of the Grounds" at Wernersville. Every afternoon, novices were sent out to work on the property to perform tasks like cutting grass, clipping hedges, polishing statues, digging graves, shoveling snow, and cleaning the swimming pool. The Jesuit priest overseeing work of this kind was Dominic Hammer, who also taught Latin and Greek to novices. I still have his two little paperback books, *Aids to Greek Grammar* and *Latin Etymology*. Also tending to the grounds keeping was an elderly layman, Oscar Beaky, and it was to him that I reported. His office was the second, and top, floor of a car barn at the edge of our property. I used to go up there and check with Oscar about the work I should be assigning to my fellow novices. Listening to Oscar's advice was a genuinely profitable education, and we became very good friends. One day he invited me to ride home with him for dinner, which his wife was preparing.

Unbeknownst to my fellow Jesuits—and my Superiors—I accepted Oscar's invitation and had a delightful dinner and evening with the two. After he drove me home, I reported this experience to our Novice Master, John ("Tex") McEvoy, who, to my great relief, smiled and nodded.

The two years that followed the novitiate were also at Wernersville, on the opposite side of the building. Those two years were the "juniorate," during which we studied Latin, Greek, and English literature, as well as religion.

In 1950, after completing my studies at Wernersville, I was assigned to a Jesuit house of studies in West Baden, Indiana, for three years of study in philosophy, both classical and contemporary, as well as in history and English literature. It was also an opportunity to get to know many Jesuits from other Jesuit provinces, including those in the Midwest. One was John O'Malley, from the Chicago Province. When I arrived and entered the living room of the building, I met John, who was reading notices on a bulletin board. He greeted and led me graciously on an impromptu tour of several common rooms on the first floor. John's specialty these days is the religious culture of early modern Europe. Another Jesuit I met and befriended was Joseph Tetlow, from the New Orleans Province, who would become founding executive secretary of the U.S. Jesuit Conference but who at West Baden would become the top tenor of a barbershop quartet that I initiated! Joe would recall decades later that during those years I taught him "all about East Coast elbow-in-eye basketball."

The building at West Baden—a hotel converted into a seminary—was huge and circular with an enormous and beautifully designed center. Outside my window on the other side was a swimming pool followed by a small golf course. Besides our classes and academic projects, we were also encouraged to dress in lay attire and visit families in the small town near our property. Unfortunately, and understandably, many of these people were hardly thrilled about the Jesuits taking over the former hotel, which went out of business a little over a decade earlier and had created jobs and other economic activity for the small town. As a religious order with the vow of poverty, the Jesuits could not provide the same economic function. But relationships did warm over time, and the three families I visited eventually became close friends of mine.

When I completed my studies at West Baden in 1953, I was assigned to what we call "Regency." A "regent" is a "teacher," and for three years, I taught Latin, English, and religion to seniors at Gonzaga College High School in Washington, D.C. I also taught a course in Greek literature, Xenophon's *Anabasis*, to a class of juniors. Many of these students, some of whom became very influentially and profitably employed, are still good friends of mine.

After Regency I was assigned to theology studies at the Jesuit School of Theology in Weston, Massachusetts. In my third year at Weston, I was ordained to the priesthood there on June 13, 1959. Upon completing our four years of theology, we did a year of "Tertianship" during which we were directed—as a group—through a full 30-day retreat of the Ignatian Spiritual Exercises, followed by eight months of spiritual direction from the Tertian Director. We also celebrated daily Mass for neighbors in a large chapel on campus and brought sacramental service to members of various neighboring parishes.

Next stop: Rome

3.

In Rome, On the Verge of Vatican II

At the Gregorian, 1961-1963

After Tertianship, I was sent to Rome for three years to get a doctoral degree in theology at the Gregorian University. All of the classes were taught in Latin, and the written tests and oral exams were in Latin as well. My doctoral dissertation, on the other hand, was penned in English, albeit with a partial, Latin title: *Gratia Capitis Christi* [The Grace of Christ's Headship]: *Its Nature and Function According to Saint Thomas Aquinas.*

It was an intense few years of academic work, but I had some experiences apart from studies and scholarship. For one thing, I was allowed to travel through Europe, England, and Ireland—where I began to get a taste of the variety of cultures and religious experiences. Back in Rome, I would say Mass every morning at the Church of St. Ignatius ("Sant' Ignazio'" for the Italians) on an altar dedicated to Robert Bellarmine, a Jesuit saint, cardinal, and master theologian during the 16th and early 17th centuries.

My classmates and I also had our favorite haunts, including the Tazzo d'Oro, or "The Cup of Gold," a café where you could get coffee from all over the world. Another haunt was the German Bierstube. In my day, Italian beer was not very good, so we used to gravitate to the few German places in town where you could get a proper brew. I remember going there with my father, along with my brother, Marty, and his wife, Ruth, when Marty gave dad a trip to Europe for his 70th birthday.

There was also no shortage of memorable Jesuit figures in Rome at that time. One of them was Felix Maria Cappello, a famous confessor at

Sant' Ignazio for the many who flocked to him in droves every Sunday morning starting around 6:00 a.m. He was one of those rare people who apparently could tell people things about themselves before they even told him. He had a miraculous insight into people, was unfailingly kind, gifted with great wisdom, and gave excellent advice in the confessional. I remember the day in 1962 when someone arrived from his residence to announce to the crowd that Cappello had died overnight. The sacristans had all they could do to keep the crowd from tearing his confessional to pieces, the way Italians might tear down a goal post for souvenirs at the end of a championship soccer game.

Visiting the church more than three decades later, I noticed a confessional that was clearly no longer in service but had a glass door in the center, through which you could see clerical attire on display: a confessional stole, a biretta, a Roman collar and other items. All of them belonged to Cappello, whose canonization cause was opened in 1987. During that long trip to Rome—where I attended the 34th General Congregation of the Society of Jesus, in 1995—I also returned to some of the old haunts, including the café and beer garden still there. And, I went back to the graduate student residence, where I saw, in the main corridor—surprise of surprises—class pictures dating from 1950 to the present. There I was, looking so young and healthy, and it was strange also to look into the faces of my classmates, a fair number of whom were fellow delegates to that General Congregation.

Getting back to the academic side of things, one of the most enduringly influential figures for me was a theology professor at the Gregorian named Bernard Lonergan. He was a Canadian Jesuit who wrote more than 25 books and made a huge mark on Catholic theology for decades to come. One of his books, which I have read over and over and have used as the principal text in theology courses I have taught, in retreats I have offered, and in meetings with business executives, is *Method in Theology*.

Chapter 4 of the book is titled "Religion," and one section of that chapter in particular has served as a major influence on me and my work for others. It deals with the question of self-transcendence, and because of its lasting impact on me and so many others, I'll quote freely from the passages.

Man achieves authenticity in self-transcendence.

One can live in a world, have a horizon, just in the measure that one is not locked up in oneself. A first step toward this liberation is the sensitivity we share with higher animals. But they are confined to a habitat, while man lives in a universe. Beyond sensitivity man asks questions, and his questioning is unrestricted.

Lonergan goes on to discuss different kinds of self-transcendence, including the intellectual sort—which involves ascending from what merely appears to me, or what I think, to what is really so. Lonergan adds that self-transcendence is not only cognitive, but also moral—in that it affects the way we live our lives and the actions we take, upon deliberation. "When we ask whether this or that is worthwhile, whether it is not just apparently good but truly good, then we are inquiring, not about pleasure or pain, not about comfort or ill ease, not about sensitive spontaneity, not about individual or group advantage, but about objective value. Because we can ask such questions, and answer them, and live by the answers, we can effect in our living a moral self-transcendence," he writes. "That moral self-transcendence is the possibility of benevolence and beneficence, of honest collaboration and true love, of swinging completely out of the habitat of an animal and of becoming a person in human society."

Love has a lot to do with this, and there are different kinds.

"There is the love of intimacy, of husband and wife, of parents and children. There is the love of one's fellow men with its fruit in the achievement of human welfare. There is the love of God with one's whole heart and whole soul, with all one's mind and all one's strength (Mark 12, 30). It is God's love flooding our hearts through the Holy Spirit given to us (Romans 5, 5). It grounds the conviction of Saint Paul that 'there is nothing in death or life, in the realm of spirits or superhuman powers, in the world as it is or the world as it shall be, in the forces of the universe, in heights or depths—nothing in all creation that can separate us from the love of God in Christ Jesus our Lord' (Romans 8:38 f.)."

Ultimately, it's about falling in love with God—unreservedly, and in total self-surrender to what God is doing in our lives:

As the question of God is implicit in all our questioning, so being in love with God is the basic fulfillment of our conscious intentionality. That fulfillment brings a deep-set joy that can remain despite humiliation, failure, privation, pain, betrayal, desertion. That fulfillment brings a radical peace, the peace that the world cannot give. That fulfillment bears fruit in a love of one's neighbor that strives mightily to bring about the kingdom of God on this earth. On the other hand, the absence of that fulfillment opens the way to trivialization of human life in the pursuit of fun, to the harshness of human life arising from the ruthless exercise of power, to despair about human welfare springing from the conviction that the universe is absurd.

Lonergan's methodological insights could not have come at a more propitious time for the Church and the People of God. Vatican II was upon us, and the Church was throwing open its window to the modern world, placing a greater value on human experience and the urgent need to read the signs of the times. For me, Lonergan's method served as a tool for helping people in their own processes of discernment, helping to reflect on their experiences, what is really so, and what God is calling them to do. It is a process that would speak volumes also about the Jesuit way of proceeding. Business professionals, diplomats, Church professionals, lay collaborators in Jesuit mission, and many others would benefit from this methodology.

But first, we had to get through the 1960s.

4.

Theology in the Streets— and a Life-Changing Experience

Loyola College, Baltimore, 1963 to 1968

Wrapping up in Rome, I was assigned to Loyola College (now Loyola University Maryland) in Baltimore. I served as a professor of theology at Loyola for six years, starting in 1963, teaching members of the senior class. That last year, 1968, was one of the most tumultuous in modern American history: assassinations and other upheavals left their marks on campus as well as society.

In June 1968, Robert F. Kennedy was gunned down in Los Angeles, just as the presidential contender was emerging victorious from the always pivotal California Democratic primary. RFK had evolved into a champion of causes on behalf of economic and racial justice, and likewise came to oppose the Vietnam War. He was just 42 years old. A little earlier that spring, the Rev. Dr. Martin Luther King Jr. was fatally shot in Memphis, after answering a call to support a strike by the city's sanitation workers. He was just 39. At the time, King and his Southern Christian Leadership Conference had been planning a march on Washington to demand a more serious national response to the plight of the poor in our country.

The King assassination triggered riots across much of the urban map of the United States, adding to the already thick racial tensions in cities such as Baltimore. The mayor of Baltimore insisted that we Jesuits and Loyola students not go out after 5:00 p.m. when the city was under strict police surveillance. If I did need to go out for priestly service, I would make sure to wear my black suit and Roman collar, and I made it very clear to the police that there was an important pastoral need that I had to tend to.

Clearly the world was in chaos in 1968, so the Loyola College seniors and I basically said to each other, "We ought to organize a series of programs and activities to meet the needs of today." We started a group called Loyola Students for Social Action (LSSA), guided by two students who were blood brothers, John and Francis Knott, with me as faculty moderator. They initiated a number of programs and practices, including reading and discussion groups for students, faculty, and parents, service to those with intellectual disabilities, recreation for low-income children, volunteer work in the pediatric wards of local hospitals, and other activities.

Frequently, they and others would take further steps. African American students, for example, would go to bars and restaurants where they were unwelcome on account of the color of their skin, sit down and attempt to order something in an effort to break down the barriers of segregation. Sometimes they got thrown out; occasionally they "converted" the previously biased staff members of the restaurant or bar. For many, it was faith in action, theology in the streets.

"Jim, It's Time to Go Home"

I had another, and actually life-changing, experience at Loyola College.

It happened one evening in the dining room of our Jesuit community residence at Loyola College. I had gotten up and was walking toward the dining room door when I heard a voice in my head saying very clearly: "Jim, it's time to go home. You have been at boarding school long enough!" I was shocked. "It's time to go home! What does it mean—go back to live with my parents in Philadelphia? Hardly!" It took me a while to figure out what in the world "going home" meant. Gradually it came to me that though we Jesuits were good friends, enjoyed our camaraderie, and liked our work, we really were not deeply bonded in a solid Jesuit foundation. We were more like a group of diocesan priests who put "S.J." after our names. We did not share a sense of clear identity as a Jesuit brotherhood. Our roots were so shallow that we could not verbalize and describe to ourselves or others what it was to be a Jesuit priest.

That experience was a vocational crisis for me. Was "going home" a call to leave the Society of Jesus? Well, at least, I thought, I should search for a possible answer. And search I did. I read, I prayed, I consulted others—and finally it dawned upon me. What bonds and identifies us as Jesuits is a particular type of spirituality that St. Ignatius received from God and then bequeathed to his companions in a retreat called "Spiritual Exercises." That spirituality gives identity, focus and direction to us and to our mission. The Exercises provide a methodology for discerning what, in the concrete, God is asking of us here and now, and it motivates us to forgo self-interest in order to be compassionately concerned for the service of others. It is a vision, mission, motivation, and methodology for service—all in companionship with Jesus who is alive and collaborating with us, and inviting us to live lives of collaboration with him.

The light went on! "Coming home" meant a return to the Spiritual Exercises as the bedrock of Jesuit spirituality, guidance, and systematic belief and behavior on our mission with and for others.

Six months later, I was leading the Maryland Province of the Society of Jesus.

5.

A Sudden Call

Provincial Superior of the Maryland Province of
Jesuits, 1968 to 1973

In early July of 1968, I had just returned home from two weeks at the New Jersey shore with several Jesuit friends and had gone down to my office in the basement of our Jesuit residence to start organizing material for upcoming fall courses. The phone rang and when I picked it up I was told, "Jim, this is Father Hugh Kennedy." He was the *socius* (executive assistant) to the provincial.

He asked me, "Where are you?"

I said, "In my office."

He asked, "Are you alone and is the office door closed?"

I said, "Yes."

Then he said, "I want you to know that our four Province Consultors agreed upon three Jesuits who might be good provincials. You were one of the three. We sent that proposal over to Father General [Pedro Arrupe, in Rome] with the request that unless he chooses you we would like him to send the list back so we could develop another list. Today we have just gotten word back that Father General has chosen you as the next provincial of the Maryland Province."

He went on to tell me that, since our previous provincial had resigned from the job very abruptly for personal reasons, an appointment had to be made quickly. He told me to resign from the Loyola College faculty and to report to the provincial's office in mid-July.

I was stunned. I had no administrative experience. I was 39 years old. And I knew very few Jesuits in the Maryland Province, since almost all my studies had been done in other provinces in the U.S. and abroad. Moreover, the Maryland Province was in shock and deeply divided over the abrupt resignation of its former provincial, Ed Sponga. As I later learned, he had written a note and slipped it under Kennedy's bedroom door at midnight. It said, "Hugh, by the time you are reading this note I will have left the Society of Jesus and the priesthood, and will probably already be married."

This was the Maryland Province that I was being asked to lead.

When I took over the job, I could see immediately that the confusion about identity that I had experienced in my Jesuit life was widespread throughout the Society of Jesus. With some reading and reflection, I discovered that the whole Jesuit order had lost its genuine sense of identity when the Society of Jesus had been suppressed, i.e., put out of existence, by order of Pope Clement XIV. The Pope did so in 1773 under pressure from secular rulers who regarded the Jesuits as too international, too strongly and directly allied to the papacy, and too independent of the monarchs in whose territory they operated. Jesuits continued to exist as "Jesuit" only in Prussia and Russia because the monarchs of those countries valued Jesuit education. Elsewhere, the suppression lasted until 1814—for 41 years—during which time Jesuit life, tradition, and spirituality were practically lost. And all the way up to 1968, when I became provincial, much of the early Jesuit "spirit" and "spirituality" had not been recovered. For instance, individually directed retreats of the Spiritual Exercises (as distinct from the "preached" retreats for groups of Jesuits) were unknown in America.

In my early days and weeks as provincial, I started sharing with others what I had come to learn. I did it in public talks to Jesuits and our lay companions. I wrote circular letters to the Jesuit communities [the first "Dear Brothers in Christ" letter to the entire Maryland Province is excerpted in Part III, Chapter 26]. But I also gathered a half-dozen or so Jesuits who themselves had begun to see the light. And, of even greater importance, one or two of them who had studied in England or France had made those "directed" retreats of the Spiritual Exercises and therefore were able to direct others—one on one—through the retreat of the Exercises. They developed a series of conferences, workshops, articles, and in-service renewal experiences for their fellow Jesuits.

Directed retreats of the Spiritual Exercises and classes explaining the Jesuit principles underlying the Exercises gradually caught on. More and more Jesuits were making the retreats. Things settled down and our members rallied around our core "foundation." The Province community felt galvanized, energized, and purposeful.

This was all of God's doing when I heard the voice that night at dinner, "You have been at boarding school long enough. It is time to go home." It was God—through my reading, my praying, and my consulting—who brought me home. And "home" was not a place, but a vocation: a Jesuit state of mind, soul, and affection for serving others. What I learned to see and to share in those days is what I have been trying to do all the rest of my Jesuit life.

Meeting Pedro Arrupe—"I Trust You."

One of the first phone calls I received when I sat down at my desk in the Province headquarters was from Rome. It was the first assistant to our Father General, Vincent O'Keefe, of the New York Province. Vinnie told me that Father General wanted me to come to Rome to talk with him. "How about I come in a month or two—after I have had time to get the lay of the land and learn what is happening in the Province?" I suggested. "No, he wants you to come NOW," was the unequivocal answer Vinnie gave me.

So, I made my reservations and flew over to Rome within a day or two. When I arrived at the General's Residence—which I knew well from my student days in Rome—Vinnie told me that Father General would like to see me in his office the following day at 9:00 a.m. So that next morning when I knocked on the General's office door, I was shaking in my boots. The door opened and our Father General, Pedro Arrupe, was standing there looking at me, and he said, holding his hand up against my chest, "Before you come in and sit down there is something I want to tell you. And if there is nothing else you learn in the several days you are here, it will have made your whole trip eminently worthwhile. What I want you to know is this: 'I TRUST YOU!!!'"

He went on to say, "Given the turmoil in our world today, you may occasionally feel that you must make certain decisions quickly, even decisions that are actually reserved to the General. If you feel you should do it, then DO it! And if there is ever a time when you feel that I am not supporting you, I want you to pick up the phone, reverse the charges, and call me immediately—because the one thing we cannot tolerate in the Society of Jesus today is a lack of trust and confidence in one another!"

Wow! I knew at that moment that I would walk on burning coals for that man. His trust engendered in me a profound and lasting trust in and for him—and for the Jesuit ideals he represented. That's true LEADERSHIP! And that was Pedro—through his whole life. He was also very humble, very prayerful, almost monastic in his morning meditation. He would kneel down on the floor and hunch back, very much like a monk in the desert. He engendered that same feeling among other people. We got to be very good friends, and I would go over there frequently as provincial and later as president of the U.S. Jesuit Conference. Pedro Arrupe is now on the road to canonization, but he has always been a saint, in my book.

Hugh Kennedy, my "second in command," or *socius*, who had held that job under several previous provincials, taught me a valuable lesson early on about "listening." He said to me one day, "Jim, I think it is time for you to hit the road and start visiting the Jesuits in their communities."

"Don't you think I ought to wait a while, Hugh?" I asked him. "Until I learn the job a little better, I don't think I have anything to say to them."

"Jim," Kennedy responded, "the men are not the slightest bit interested in what you have to say to them. All they are interested in is that you listen to what they have to say to you." That was one of the wisest things I have ever been told.

As provincial, I visited every year with each member of each community in the Maryland Province for at least forty-five minutes. This served as a "manifestation of conscience" and it enabled the two of us to get to know one another in a very interpersonal way. This enabled me to propose new assignments to certain Jesuits with genuinely mutual satisfaction—even some that were quite different than what either of us expected.

I also had an opportunity to share my experiences with—and learn greatly from—the nine other U.S. Jesuit provincials, individually and as a group. I told them of my "conversion," that is, the realization of how our Jesuit identity is rooted in the graces, the vision, and the mission of the Spiritual Exercises of Saint Ignatius. I would get to know them and the broader Jesuit world even better, during my next appointment, in Washington, D.C.

6.

From Provincial to President

National Jesuit Conference,
1973 to 1981

When my six-year term as provincial came to an end, I joined the staff of the National Jesuit Conference (now, the Jesuit Conference of Canada and the United States) and within three years was appointed president of the Conference. It too was a six-year term, during which time I visited and counseled the U.S. provincials individually, while gathering all of them together periodically for an exercise of "communal discernment" on key issues of apostolic importance that we all faced in the United States.

Likewise, Father General Pedro Arrupe would invite me to come to Rome to meet with six other presidents of national Jesuit Conferences around the world. Our conversations together gave me an understanding of, and an appreciation for, the worldwide influence and apostolic value of the graces of the Spiritual Exercises. This was the very core of our Jesuit existence and apostolates.

During my years at the Jesuit Conference, I came to know many lay people in Washington, D.C. My office was just off DuPont Circle and the Brookings Institution was practically next door. Brookings is a non-profit public policy organization whose mission is to conduct in-depth research that leads to new ideas for solving problems facing society at the local, national, and global levels. I got to meet and know many of the people at Brookings. One of them, Anthony Downs, a senior fellow with a doctorate in economics from Stanford University and author or coauthor of 27 books, became a very good friend and would invite me to monthly luncheons at Brookings with other influential corporate and financial leaders in Washington. Eventually, Tony started coming to me for spiritual direction, as did other Brookings members. We were learning a lot from one another as we bonded.

Also, while I was at the Jesuit Conference, I had come to know a very active and influential group of Holy Trinity parishioners, namely, the members of the Social Concerns Committee. Holy Trinity is the Jesuit parish located just outside the gates of Georgetown University, and the collaboration started one afternoon when I was in my office and received a phone call from a Holy Trinity parishioner, Paul McElligott, asking if he could visit me in my office. It was a hectic time for me, and with a bit of reluctance, I said, "fine," and we settled on a day and time. When he came, he said that the Social Concerns Committee was going to make a weekend retreat at a Jesuit retreat house in Maryland, and they would like for me to be their retreat director. I thanked him for this gracious invitation but said I was really too busy to do it. Three days later he phoned me again with the same request and, once again, I had to decline. Not to be deterred, after another three days, Paul phoned me yet again, and out of sheer exasperation I said, "Alright, alright! When and where is it going to be?" He told me that it would be at Manresa, the retreat house right across the bay from the U.S. Naval Academy.

At the retreat I gave points for meditation twice a day, morning and afternoon, and I told the retreatants to let me know if they'd like to visit with me in my office for counseling or confession. Most of them did come to see me, so I got to know them quite well. At the end of the retreat we had a "Bon Voyage" celebration. Little did any of us know that my next Jesuit assignment would be as pastor of Holy Trinity Parish! This retreat in the fall of 1979 was the first of nine that I would direct for the Social Concerns Committee.

In the spring of 1980, I travelled to El Salvador to participate in the March 30 funeral of Archbishop (now Saint) Oscar Romero. A legendary advocate for the poor, he was martyred while celebrating Mass in the chapel of the Hospital of Divine Providence. My heart has always been with social justice and this experience was particularly influential in connecting my heart to the social apostolate. I remember the day vividly and excerpt below an article I wrote for *America* magazine, dated April 26, 1980:

The funeral ceremonies started calmly on a beautiful, but hot day. A procession of some 30 bishops (from England, Ireland, Spain, Canada, Mexico, Brazil, Ecuador, Peru, Venezuela, Honduras, Nicaragua, Guatemala, Panama, Costa Rica, and the United States) and more than 200 priests wound its way through eight or ten blocks of the city from the church where we had vested to the cathedral. Hundreds of people lined the sidewalks, many of them listening to a radio broadcast of the event on their transistor radios. We had been assured that the day would be peaceful and free of "events." The Popular Front, including the far left, had covenanted to observe nonviolence in honor of the archbishop, and it seemed unthinkable that the hard-line right would desecrate this moment unless first provoked.

At first, all went as promised. The bishops and clergy processed into the cathedral through a side door, went out the front door to salute the altar set up in front of the cathedral, and then moved to our assigned places. The clergy remained inside the front door of the cathedral while the bishops stood outside on the altar platform and faced the square. The entire plaza was filled with more than 100,000 persons, and thousands more spilled over into the side streets leading to it.

All went peacefully through a succession of prayers, readings, hymns until the moment in his homily when Cardinal Ernesto Corripio Ahumada of Mexico, the personal delegate of Pope John Paul II, began to praise Archbishop Romero as a man of peace and a foe of violence. Suddenly, a bomb exploded at the far edge of the plaza, seemingly in front of the National Palace, a government building. Next, gun shots, sharp and clear, echoed off the walls surrounding the plaza. At first, the cardinal's plea for all to remain calm seemed to have a steadying impact. But as another explosion reverberated, panic took hold and the crowd broke ranks and ran. Some headed for the side streets, but thousands more rushed up the stairs and fought their way into the cathedral.

As one of the concelebrating priests, I had been inside the cathedral from the start. Now I watched the terrified mob push through the doors until every inch of space was filled. Looking about me, I suddenly realized that, aside from the nuns, priests and bishops, the mourners were the poor and the powerless of El Salvador. Absent were government representatives of the nation or of other countries. The ceremony had begun at 11 a.m. and it was now after noon. For the next hour and a half or two, we found ourselves tightly packed into the cathedral, some huddled under the pews, others clutching one another in fright, still others praying silently or aloud.

The bomb explosions grew closer and more frequent until the cathedral began to shudder. Would the whole edifice collapse? Or would a machine gunner appear in a doorway to strafe the crowd? A little peasant girl named Reina, dressed up in her brown-and-white checked Sunday dress, clung to me in desperation and pleaded, "Padre."

We lived through that horror of bombs, bullets and panic, now dead bodies were being carried into the cathedral from outside, for nearly two hours. At certain moments one could not help wondering if we would all be killed. At the same time, I was already asking myself, "What is going on here? What is this experience telling me about the debate between Archbishop Romero and the U.S. State Department?"

Eventually, the bombing and shooting subsided. The papal nuncio to El Salvador received assurance by phone from some government source that it was safe for the people to leave the cathedral. Gradually, we filed out into the street with hands raised high above our heads, according to instructions, so as to assure any potential snipers that we were unarmed.

Later in the afternoon, back at the Jesuit residence where I was staying, we listened by radio to the Government's official account of the incident. The entire affair, the statement explained, was the work of leftist terrorists. Our own experience had given us, of course, a different picture....

Social analysis, they say, depends basically on your starting point: from where and with whom you view the social situation. As I sat huddled in the San Salvador cathedral with thousands of terrified peasants, I found myself viewing the Salvadoran social situation with the poor and from their perspective of weakness, terror, and oppression. I was given a vivid experience of the power of evil that can permeate the institutions and behavior of those who fight to uphold an unjust system. That experience helped greatly to sharpen and put disparate pieces in order....

When my term as president of the Jesuit Conference was completed, the provincial of the Maryland Province assigned me as pastor of Holy Trinity. Having already come to know many parishioners from the Social Concerns retreats, I felt at the time that it was a graced assignment, and it turned out to be very graced indeed.

7.
From President to Pastor

Holy Trinity Parish, 1981 to 1987

I guess I shouldn't have been surprised when I stepped into the sanctuary of Holy Trinity to celebrate my first Mass as pastor, and looked out on the congregation to see the first three rows of pews filled with familiar faces—members of the Social Concerns Committee! As they say, we picked up the ball and ran from there, in service to the poor and socially marginalized of the District of Columbia. Holy Trinity had already bonded with Saint Aloysius Jesuit Parish ("St. Al's"), where the legendary Horace McKenna was serving as pastor, in a somewhat marginal neighborhood near Capitol Hill. Horace was well known as a "priest of the poor."

The day I moved into the rectory of Holy Trinity, I had no sooner sat down in my office when the phone rang. I picked it up and heard a familiar voice say, "Jim, this is Horace McKenna. Welcome to parish life!" And he hung up immediately. Of course, I had known Horace very well over the years and was familiar with his tireless work with the inner-city poor of the nation's capital. When I was provincial and met with Horace for his annual "manifestation," he refused to sit in an office and talk. Rather, we would walk around the neighborhood and he would greet everyone by name, warmly welcomed into the homes of those he served. Oftentimes, we would just sit on a street corner with those who had no homes. During my visits with him, I became intimately acquainted with Horace's character, his dedication, his ministry, and his sanctity.

It was the twilight of Horace's ministry on earth. A year after I arrived at Holy Trinity, I was preaching the homily at his funeral Mass at St. Al's, on Saturday, May 15, 1982. There were more than a thousand people gathered, and among them, at the back of the church, sat a group of street people. They had come to pay their respects to the priest they loved who had died four days earlier. My homily was based on a handwritten summary of Horace's life, which Horace had prepared nearly seven years earlier. In Horace's "Personal Odyssey," he frequently used the word "integration," and I thought the word was a characterization of Horace, since he had given his life "for integration, for reconciliation, for the unity of love among all people." Like Jesus, as described by Saint Paul, Horace had broken down the barrier of division and had destroyed hostility.

"Look around you," I said. "What do you see in this congregation, this gathering of people? We see rich and we see poor; we see blacks and we see whites; we see men and women—of every segment of our society. And why are we here? What has drawn us together? . . . We are bound together in our love and affection for him, for Father Horace. We are one today because of him. In his own person, he had broken down lines, barriers, and distinctions between us. He is—at this moment—our reconciler, mediator, and peacemaker. He has been the door through which so many of us pass to friendship with one another. Our tribute to him must be a pledge to strengthen that friendship with one another, to rededicate ourselves to integration, to continue his work with the poor, and to reverence the Gospel which he read. As we say 'Yes' to him, we say 'Yes' in our own lives to all he stood and lived for."

To this day, I keep on my desk a picture of Horace and myself sitting side by side at a Holy Trinity Social Concerns Committee meeting, and I often remember something he once wrote and imagined, with complete honesty: "When God lets me into heaven, I think I'll ask to go off in a corner somewhere for half an hour and sit down and cry because the strain is off, the work is done, and I haven't been unfaithful or disloyal, all these needs that I have known are in the hands of Providence and I don't have to worry any longer who's at the door, whose breadbox is empty, whose baby is sick, whose home is shaken and discouraged, and whose children can't read," he wrote. I think the key words here were "in the hands of Providence."

Thomas P. Gavigan, who had been pastor at Holy Trinity parish from 1964 to 1970, also welcomed me warmly upon my arrival and at the time was serving as pastor emeritus. Tom can legitimately be called "the second founder of Holy Trinity Church" because he was pastor immediately after the Second Vatican Council and successfully introduced all of the many changes in parish life that were demanded by the Council. He later said in a parish publication, "One of the great insights of Vatican II is that the people are the Church. It's not the vast organization, the hierarchy and the clergy, it's the people. I thank God for the people of Holy Trinity. They are truly the People of God!"

At 71 years young, Tom continued to celebrate daily Mass, visit the homebound in the parish, officiate at baptisms, weddings and funerals, take phone calls day and night from anyone in need, and provide encouragement and support to his fellow Jesuits and lay staff alike. He became a trusted mentor and cherished friend to me.

Early on in my days as pastor, someone asked me what I planned to change in the parish. I replied, "I have decided to listen for a year before I change anything." Moreover, my motto on arrival was, "Power to the People," i.e., the people in the pews, the people who are Holy Trinity. My subtitle to that motto was, "Less work for Father." Actually, the work wasn't less, but different. It was the role of a traffic cop. I tried to help all of these very active parishioners, including committee chairs, stay in communication and on parallel tracks with each other, so as to avoid crashes at intersections. All of the things that happened during my tenure as pastor happened thanks to parish "People Power."

I felt particularly privileged and blessed to be at this parish to celebrate a milestone in April 1987. It was a joyous celebration of the 200th anniversary of the founding of Holy Trinity. The Bicentennial Steering Committee, co-chaired by Anne and Milan Miskovsky, planned a year-long celebration that began on October 4, 1986, with the inaugural event titled "A Day in Old Georgetown." The opening ceremony at 2:00 p.m. featured the U.S. Navy Band and the U.S. Marine Corps Color Guard. The day included antique autos on display, historical artifact booths, children's games, music provided by the St. Aloysius Church Choir along with the Alumni Georgetown University Chimes, "Living History" presentations, a special liturgy on the church steps, and an old-fashioned church supper. After the meal, a country music band played and parishioners danced on N Street. The evening culminated with the illumination of the façade of the original church (used as a parish office at the time) and an ecumenical bell ringing by Georgetown churches. It was a wonderful day to bring in a year of celebration—and reflection on the past, present, and future of Holy Trinity. The opening event was primarily coordinated by Alice and Raymond Pushkar, members of the steering committee.

The next special event to mark the parish bicentennial was a workshop held at Georgetown Visitation Convent on October 25, 1986, to discuss a book compiled and edited by parishioners. The title of this book, *As The Father Has Sent Me*, is taken from the Gospel reading for Sunday, April 26, 1987, on which Holy Trinity officially celebrated its bicentennial. It was providential that this particular Scripture passage coincided with our Bicentennial Sunday, because it captures much of what that year meant for parishioners.

As I said in the preface to the book, "There are so many gifts in our history for which we are grateful. But it is also a time to take stock, a time to discern where God is leading us." And what does it mean—for followers of Jesus—to "take stock"?

> The yardstick for Christian "stock taking" is the vitality of our service to others. As a Christian community we are on the mission of Jesus. The bicentennial is an opportunity for us to rededicate ourselves to that mission. To be part of the mission of Jesus, we must be in service, as best we can, to all people. Jesus came, he said, not to be served, but to serve, and the greatest of all, He taught his disciples, is the one who serves others.
>
> To rededicate ourselves to that we must pray. The bicentennial year, therefore, is planned as a year of prayer and service. This book, a collection of prayerful reflections and service opportunities, is the principal tool that we will use to guide us through our year.

Parishioners were given a one-page guide to the weekly scriptural prayers and reflections along with tips for using the book. In addition, they were encouraged to participate in the service opportunities described in the third part of the book. There were monthly service projects as well as opportunities to serve more frequently at organizations in Washington, helping the homeless, the hungry, the elderly, and others in need. The service projects were coordinated by Ruth Connor, my sister-in-law, who gave countless hours for many years to the Social Concerns Committee.

A follow-up workshop on "As the Father Has Sent Me" took place a year later on April 25, 1987, and parishioners gathered to reflect on their prayer and service experiences together. There was also a special bicentennial lecture series featuring distinguished theologians and Church historians like Monika Hellwig, John Tracy Ellis, and Gerald P. Fogarty, S.J., among others.

Another important facet of the bicentennial was a project undertaken by parishioner and author William W. Warner to write the history of Holy Trinity and its place in the growth of the Federal City. A former administrator at the Smithsonian Institution, he had won the Pulitzer Prize for nonfiction in 1977 for his *Beautiful Swimmers: Watermen, Crabs and the Chesapeake Bay*, a blend of history, ecology, and anthropology. Known to his friends as Willie, the plan was to complete the volume during the bicentennial year. However, Willie said that my request to write the history of Holy Trinity set him off on an inviting journey towards a much larger goal. So the project spilled over not only the bicentennial year but also my tenure as pastor.

After several years of intense research and writing, *At Peace with all Their Neighbors: Catholics and Catholicism in the National Capital, 1787-1860*, was published by Georgetown University Press in October 1994. To facilitate Willie's efforts, I was able to offer him an office at the Woodstock Theological Center at Georgetown University, which was my next assignment after Holy Trinity. Willie said in the "Acknowledgments" section of his book that having me at close hand was "a constant source of encouragement, advice, and good cheer." But in fact, the pleasure was all mine. Willie was a masterful raconteur, wonderful storyteller, and treasured friend. I preached at his funeral at Holy Trinity in April of 2008.

On Sunday, April 26, 1987, bicentennial liturgies were celebrated all morning and followed by receptions. There were numerous distinguished guests, among them Cardinal James A. Hickey of Washington, D.C.; James A. Devereux, provincial of the Maryland Province of Jesuits; and Georgetown University's Jesuit president, Timothy S. Healy. In my "Reminiscences, Hopes and Blessings," published in the bicentennial book, I offered:

Under God's guidance, something very good and special is happening at Holy Trinity parish. Some indications: people come here to "return to the church"; an extraordinary number of people participate actively in the life and activities of this parish and many more want to; people are hungry for religious education and spiritual growth; people praise their experience of community at Holy Trinity and work to build up relationships of friendship and mutual support; people are very generous in giving money, food, clothing, and so on to the poor and needy, and some give also of their time; there is the sense among very many that this is "their" parish: that here they have a "home" of respectful and caring friends in a world which is busy, calculating, and driven to achieve.

In all of this God is blessing us richly by giving us the lived experience of the Christian life. We feel the challenges and the rewards. We're alive. The Spirit is alive in us.

What is my main hope for the future? Our U.S. culture and society show signs of demoralization, cynicism, even despair, leading people to "grab it" (pleasure, money, power, whatever) now at any cost. This makes us dangerous to ourselves and to others. It is not just a personal affliction; it has become "environmental." It is a widespread epidemic of depression.

We come to Holy Trinity as the counter-balance to this oppressive environment and these alienating relationships. But what can Trinity do to reach out and minister to our poor, ailing world? How do we reach people and the social environment with the GOOD NEWS of hope for the future, confidence in oneself, peace within, and the fear-free capacity to forgive—even enemies?

"As the Father has sent me, so I send you!'" is the theme of our Bicentennial. How, concretely, are we being sent into this complex, suffering world of ours? It is my hope that we can come to clearer grips with this vocation.

And God bless us all.

A couple of months later, on Trinity Sunday in 1987, the parish celebrated its feast day with the annual picnic on the grounds of the nearby Visitation Convent. Liturgy began at 10:30 a.m. followed by fun, food, games, and entertainment. I was wrapping up my time at Holy Trinity, and was given a wonderful and memorable sendoff by parishioners. Many of them have remained lifelong friends and collaborators in my future apostolates.

Perhaps the highlight of the entertainment at the picnic was a stand up "monologue" delivered by Nita Crowley. Nita was on the first retreat I gave to the Social Concerns Committee in 1979, and during my years at Trinity, she headed up the committee while also serving on the Parish Council. By day, Nita was a very accomplished attorney at a prestigious Washington law firm, and was at all times a very witty person. She continued to be a treasured friend and colleague, serving on the Board of Directors at Woodstock for several years.

On top of that, Nita became known as my official "roaster" over the years. At Holy Trinity, I often extolled the "pancake" image of the Church—authority, power, and responsibility spread out among the laity. When she roasted me at the end of my pastorate, Nita observed, "There is never just one pancake on the plate. And I know who the top pancake is!" Afterward, whenever I was celebrating a special anniversary or receiving an award from an organization like the Loyola Retreat House or the Ignatian Solidarity Network, Nita would be there to offer her hilarious perspective on it all for me.

* * *

In May of 1987, as I prepared to step down as pastor, I was interviewed by Holy Trinity parishioner and journalist Bill Steponkus. I remember telling him that what most surprised me about the job as pastor was the variety of activities, ranging from weighty CEO matters typical of a corporate executive to serious, one-on-one counseling. It's like being the president, principal, and teacher at a high school all at the same time.

In that same interview, I was asked to list accomplishments, and I told him I'd rather talk about things "for which to be grateful," things that resulted from collaborative efforts among many parishioners. At the top of my list was the introduction of Scripture-based prayer groups in parishioner homes, which began in Advent and Lent of 1984-85 and flourished under the leadership of devoted parishioners Jim and Karen Nolan and Grace and Jack O'Connor.

Second on my list was bringing Jerry Campbell, S.J., former Georgetown University president, to Holy Trinity to establish the Center for Ignatian Spirituality, offering the retreat of the Spiritual Exercises in its Annotation 19 form, and then training others to direct these retreats. The Center was funded by a generous contribution from Marie G. Wanek, a parishioner and professor of Asian studies, who lived one block from the church. Natalie Ganley and Ellen Crowley worked closely with Jerry in launching and helping to train many others to direct retreats. I mentioned other things "for which to be grateful," having to do with many aspects of parish life.

I will always look back on my years at Holy Trinity as the richest time in my life, a time when I had the opportunity to share with parishioners the whole range of human experience.

8.
Getting to Woodstock

Woodstock Theological Center, Georgetown University,
1987-2002

Back in 1973, the Jesuit provincials of New York and Maryland announced that they had "decided to inaugurate a center for theological reflection as a new ministry" of those provinces, the purpose of which would be to promote such reflection "in the Roman Catholic tradition, but with openness to dialogue with other traditions and disciplines." There was a need, the provincials added, for "a new development in theological method, which speaks clearly to the current situation."

That role would be served by the Woodstock Theological Center, founded in 1974 after a long process of investigation, consultation, and reflection about how best to reorient the resources of Woodstock College, the Jesuit seminary, which closed in 1974. Eamon G. Taylor, the New York provincial, and J. A. Panuska, the Maryland provincial, made the announcement in a letter dated November 19, 1973. Referring to Pedro Arrupe, they said, "We hope this Center will respond to Father General's call for 'theological reflection on the human problems of today,' e.g., national and world justice, power, population, environment, consumerism, etc."

The provincials located the Center in Washington, D.C., because, "We have solid reasons to believe that Washington—as the home of governmental policy and of so many economic and social agencies, together with the strengths afforded by the cooperative presence of Georgetown University and Catholic University—will provide a suitable ambience and valuable network of relationships for the Center's work. And we are mindful of the presence of the Catholic Bishops' Conference and many other organizations and institutes which could nourish the Center's interdisciplinary needs and afford it broad field for service to the Church, the Nation, and the world."

The two provincials then set up a committee to advise them on appointments for a director and board of advisors for the Woodstock Center. Jesuit Fathers Avery Dulles, Walter Burghardt, and myself (along with a few others) joined the committee and the three of us maintained long relationships with the Center. I stepped into the role of director more than a decade later.

That was 1987. When I arrived at my office at the Woodstock Center, one of the first persons to greet me was Tim Healy, Jesuit president of Georgetown University. Woodstock's offices were in the University's Jesuit Community on the second floor of the Old Ryan Building, and Tim's office was just down the hall, so I would see him frequently. He was very supportive of the work we were doing at Woodstock and pleased to have the Woodstock Library with its valuable collection now housed within the University's Lauinger Library. Tim and I were able to forge a long-term agreement between Georgetown and the Woodstock Center to assure that office space would be provided and other support services would be made available to Woodstock from the University.

Tim left Georgetown in 1989, after thirteen years as president, to become head of the New York Public Library. All of us at Woodstock were pleased and proud that visiting Woodstock Fellow Leo J. O'Donovan, S.J., was appointed the 47th president of Georgetown University by its board of directors. Leo participated in many Woodstock programs and events over the years, so Georgetown and Woodstock continued a warm and collaborative relationship.

In those early days at Woodstock, I felt still more grateful for my time at the parish because it gave me the opportunity to be in touch with the trends and movements that were going through the minds and hearts of people in everyday life. That provided me with a firm grounding for the kind of work I would be doing at Woodstock, "theological reflection on the human problems of today." My initial goals at the Center were to recruit more fellows, increase public education programs and publications, and stabilize the Center financially with a regular annual giving program and by acquiring foundation grants for projects.

One day, sitting in my office at Woodstock, I was looking at papers, reading memos, trying to think great thoughts, and trying to plan. I received a phone call from Avery Dulles (later to be a cardinal) asking me if I were free to join him and a friend for dinner that night. "I am free and would be pleased to meet up with you," I said. And I asked, "Who is your friend?" "He is a classmate of mine from Harvard University days," Avery said, and added, "His name is Henry Owen."

At dinner that night Henry told me that he had been thinking of becoming a Catholic and wondered what the process would be. I said, "Let's get together at your convenience and we can talk about it." We met a few days later and that conversation turned out to be the first of a whole series in which I instructed Henry in the beliefs and practices of the Catholic Church. About nine months later, I received him officially into the Catholic Church with a ceremony in the small chapel at Holy Trinity Church. Dulles came down from New York to participate in Henry's reception ceremony.

During our conversations, I came to know Henry quite well and learned that he was an influential diplomat who worked in the State Department as an economic counselor specializing in international affairs under four presidents between 1946 and 1968. In 1978, President Jimmy Carter appointed him ambassador-at-large for international economic summits.

Henry, in turn, learned about the work I was undertaking at Woodstock to review serious social issues from the perspective of religious faith and to propose constructive courses of action. After I confided that I didn't know where to begin or how to proceed, Henry came to my rescue. He proposed "hostile corporate takeovers" as the social issue to address. He said the process ought to be a series of meetings with key players in the field and ethics specialists. And finally, he said, we need to issue a publication written by an author knowledgeable in economics, ethics, and religious faith. Then he told me the names of the experts we should invite in each of these fields.

So that is what we did and the result was *Ethical Considerations in Corporate Takeovers*, published by Georgetown University Press in 1990. This project launched a permanent Woodstock program area in business ethics. Using the same formula of gathering key players in fields and ethics specialists, we went on to publish: *Creating and Maintaining an Ethical Corporate Climate*, in 1990; *Ethical Considerations in the Business Aspects of Health Care*, in 1995; and *Ethical Issues in Managed Health Care Organizations*, in 1999 (all published by Georgetown University Press). Margaret Blair of the Brookings Institution served as the principal drafter—our rapporteur—for these publications, and much help came from others including John P. Langan, S.J., whose many prominent roles at Georgetown have included serving as a fellow at Woodstock and at the Kennedy Institute of Ethics.

Building on this ethics initiative, another initiative began with the name, "The Woodstock Business Conference," a national program with chapters throughout the United States bringing business leaders together regularly to discover the relevance of religious faith to business practice. (The program was coordinated by James L. Nolan, a Holy Trinity parishioner and attorney.) I was very grateful to Avery Dulles for introducing me to Henry Owen, who sparked the beginning of these initiatives at Woodstock.

Another Woodstock program, "Preaching the Just Word," was born of casual conversation with Walter Burghardt in my office one afternoon. When Walter was approaching 80 years of age, he decided to step down as editor-in-chief of *Theological Studies* after twenty-three years. His question to me was, "What should I do now?" We talked a long time and certain things seemed to come clear: first, it ought to have something to do with preaching (Walter was a preacher's preacher); second, it should also have something to do with the contemporary mission of the Society of Jesus, namely, serving faith by promoting justice; and finally, its influence should be as widespread as possible. "Think about this," Walter said. "Every Sunday in the United States thousands of preachers are speaking to millions of people in the pews. Imagine the impact for the good of society if these homilies inspired all those people to engage the serious issues of social justice and worked to heal them."

That conversation gave birth to a five-day retreat workshop called "Preaching the Just Word," which Walter and Raymond B. Kemp led. A priest of the Archdiocese of Washington, Ray had a thriving ministry among African-American Catholics in the District (and has served most recently as Special Assistant to the President at Georgetown, in addition to teaching his popular "Struggle and Transcendence" class there). Preaching the Just Word was not only a workshop to improve preaching, but a spiritual retreat to open the eyes of participants to the fact that social justice—"biblical justice," as we specified—is at the very heart of Christ's revelation and Christian faith. Scripture scholar and long-time Woodstock associate fellow John R. Donohue, S.J., was a member of the retreat team along with several others. Retreat/workshops were held in practically every diocese of the United States and as well as in Australia, Jamaica, and Canada.

Tom Reese, S.J., was already a fellow at Woodstock when I arrived and continued his study of the church, which resulted in a trilogy of books. It started with *Archbishop: Inside the Power Structure of the American Catholic Church* (1989), which told the story of how archbishops run their archdioceses. This was followed by *A Flock of Shepherds* (1992), the story of how the U.S. bishops' conference works. The final volume in the trilogy was *Inside the Vatican: The Politics and Organization of the Catholic Church* (1996), describing and analyzing the papal curia.

Since Woodstock was established as a center of theological reflection, the whole team of Woodstock fellows worked together to grasp and gain facility in the process. We met regularly to share personal reactions to readings we had done in St. Ignatius Loyola's discernment and decision-making method, as amplified and grounded for our day by the theological reflection method of Bernard Lonergan. Arising from our discussions, a book titled *The Dynamism of Desire: Bernard J.F. Lonergan, S.J., On the Spiritual Exercises of Saint Ignatius Loyola* was published by the Institute of Jesuit Sources in 2006 (with me as editor).

Perhaps our most high-profile events were the "Woodstock Forums" held three or four times a year, with summaries of the panel discussions published in the Center's quarterly newsletter, *Woodstock Report*. Forum topics were chosen on the basis of several criteria: issues related to a Woodstock project in process; an area in which a Woodstock fellow has special expertise; or a serious question of current concern for society and church.

Over the years, the forums addressed concerns ranging from conflicts in the Middle East and the woefully unfinished business of racial justice to religious pluralism and the challenge of rejuvenating American cities, as well as the values at stake in presidential elections every four years. We brought together diverse groups of people such as journalists (E.J. Dionne of the *Washington Post* frequently among them), educators (including Leo O'Donovan), politicians (among them the bowtie-wearing U.S. Sen. Paul Simon of Illinois), and plenty of theologians. Well attended, the forums were invariably covered by local and national media.

The Woodstock Library, located in the lower level of Georgetown's Lauinger Library, was used for our regular board meetings, "Evenings of Conversation," or other special events. With over 200,000 volumes and hundreds of journals and periodicals, the library is a valuable resource for professors and Woodstock fellows. Scholars come literally from around the world to make use of this research jewel. Eugene R. "Bud" Rooney, S.J., was the librarian when I arrived at Woodstock, and in 1994, Joseph N. Tylenda, S.J., took over when Bud left for an assignment in Uruguay. Joe had just returned to the United States after seven years at the Jesuit Historical Institute in Rome, where he edited an encyclopedia about the Society of Jesus.

In my view, one of the most telling forums, in November 2001, took on the crucial topic of lay-Jesuit collaboration in higher education. The question was more than academic, as illustrated earlier in the year by the naming of John "Jack" DeGioia as the first lay president of Georgetown University. He succeeded Leo O'Donovan, who was completing a 12-year term as president. DeGioia's appointment, and his background as someone deeply steeped in Jesuit spirituality turned light on the vision of collaboration outlined by the 34th Jesuit General Congregation—"GC 34"—held in 1995. *Lay-Jesuit Collaboration in Higher Education*, the full texts of that Woodstock Forum, was published by the Institute of Jesuit Sources in 2002.

More broadly, we explored the shifting nature of Church leadership, under the expert guidance of Dolores R. Leckey, a senior Woodstock fellow who formerly directed the U.S. bishops' Secretariat for Family, Laity, Children, and Youth, and who coauthored the Woodstock-produced book, *Spiritual Exercises for Church Leaders* (Paulist Press, 2003). We initiated many other projects at Woodstock, such as our four-year study involving prominent lobbyists together with ethicists, policy makers, and others. With a team headed by Edward "Ted" Arroyo, S.J., the project led to *The Ethics of Lobbying: Organized Interests, Political Power, and the Common Good*, published by Georgetown University Press. The 110-page book featured the "Woodstock Principles for the Ethical Conduct of Lobbying," a first-of-its-kind set of guidelines for all those involved in the lobbying process.

Then there was our investigation into the role of forgiveness in international relations. That initiative began with a book by a Presbyterian ethicist, titled *An Ethic for Enemies: Forgiveness in Politics*. Donald Shriver wrote the book, which I quickly read, and then I called him up to invite him to headline a Woodstock Forum on the subject, in November 1995. The forum led to the project, "Forgiveness in International Politics: Reality and Utility," which—under the direction of myself and a Woodstock fellow, Ambassador Robert T. Hennemeyer—involved a series of colloquia that assembled distinguished scholars, religious leaders, government officials, diplomats, and practitioners in the field of conflict resolution. Four reports followed, and ultimately an award-winning book published by the U.S. Catholic Conference, titled *Forgiveness in International Politics: An Alternative Road to Peace*.

Another major initiative was the Global Economy and Cultures project, which had its roots in "GC 34." I was one of 220 Jesuit members of that General Congregation in 1995, and over the course of three months in Rome, 25 of us who worked in Jesuit social research and action centers got together informally several times to share experiences and to discover whether there were any issues on which we could fruitfully collaborate. After much discussion, we settled on the globalization of the economy and its impact on cultures. I volunteered Woodstock as the coordinating agency, asking Woodstock fellow Gasper F. (Gap) Lo Biondo, S.J., to be the coordinator. Continuing through the rest of my time at Woodstock, the project became a global gathering point for Jesuits and their collaborators working on a number of issues related to globalization, and produced an array of ethnographic studies looking at the impact of this phenomenon on local cultures around the world.

One of the more interesting theological reflection projects I introduced to the Woodstock fellows grew out of my own study and fascination with the work of Jane Jacobs.

Her groundbreaking work *The Death and Life of American Cities* was an outgrowth of her canny insight into what community was all about. She saw cities as the place where differences met and where poor and rich, educated and those striving for knowledge, met in the corridors of their neighborhoods and homes. She wrote in accessible language that spoke not only to my mind but also to my heart. I thought her work could enrich our ongoing work at Woodstock to make theological reflection part of everyday life.

At the beginning of the 21st century, I read her new book *The Nature of Economies* and realized that this amazing woman (without a college degree) understood that the meaning of life was to deal with the basic question: how to live. For a good part of one year, the fellows and guests met Friday mornings to probe together the natural connections between her work and our work in bringing theological reflection to bear on the challenges of modern life. That period of collaborative study sowed the seeds for another project—after my term as director of Woodstock—which was to explore the idea of theology in and of the city. It's a project that, I believe, needs to be revisited many times. After all, the Jesuits began in a city (Rome).

In these and other projects, the focus was not principally on where we wanted to wind up—the conclusions we wanted to reach, about this or that issue. It was the method, including the process of bringing together many different kinds of people, from many different places, for theological reflection and group discernment (rooted in the patterns of discovery, discernment, decision making, and doing laid out in the Spiritual Exercises of St. Ignatius, and further mined by Bernard Lonergan in his theological method). That's part of the reason why I often said that Woodstock is "not a where, but a way."

Personally, my feelings about the efficacy of Woodstock alternated constantly between a feeling of foolish fancy and great enthusiasm. It seemed fanciful to think that a little place like Woodstock could possibly make a difference in the midst of the powerful, complex forces that are shaping our world, when so many large, wealthy institutions are struggling to make their influence felt. On the other hand, when I would recall that no one was doing quite what Woodstock was set up to do, I felt enthusiasm. I didn't know of any other free-standing center of full-time theologians who collaborated with specialists in secular fields to look seriously at the fully human (theological) implications of the major social movements in contemporary life, with a view to reforming both faith and society through the unique, dialogical methodology we used. It was an exciting experiment.

Unfortunately, I must use the past tense. Woodstock closed down some years after my tenure (the Woodstock Library continues at Georgetown University, under the direction of Leon Hooper, S.J.). Still, those of us associated with the Center have the consolation of knowing that it played a decisive role in promoting methods of theological reflection that are now happily more common among Catholic social research and justice organizations today, particularly those in the Ignatian tradition.

The vision continues!

9.

A Return to Baltimore

Provincial Assistant for Mission and Continuing Renewal, and Jesuit in Residence, Sellinger School of Business, Loyola University, 2002-2016

After 15 years at the Woodstock Theological Center, I received a phone call from Timothy Brown, who had just taken office as provincial and who was assigning me to serve as a staff member of his Maryland Province team. Tim wanted me to collaborate with layman Kevin O'Brien, director of Ignatian Partnerships, in the newly established Office of Mission and Renewal. Our goal: to provide various opportunities for people interested in enhancing the Ignatian mission in their lives.

We would conduct workshops and retreats in Ignatian spirituality, mission, and leadership to help Jesuit and lay staff members of province apostolates (parishes, high schools, universities, etc.) understand and embrace the relevance of Jesuit spirituality. The idea was to help them apply the spirituality to their daily lives and responsibilities so they could bring these gifts to the attention of their parishioners, students, and others. Service in the broadest sense is integral to this awareness. It is what drives all of Ignatian spirituality, and we underscored in these workshops that all of us are called to a better understanding of our rapidly changing world and to learn better how to respond effectively.

In 2004, the Office of Mission and Renewal launched the Magis program, which is designed to introduce lay persons to the history, spirituality, and contemporary mission of the Society of Jesus. "Magis" is the Latin word for "more," and to Jesuits it means to always seek more, to choose activities that will achieve the greater good, to engage in one's ministry with a spirit of generous excellence, and to do so for the greater glory of God—*Ad Majorem Dei Gloriam*! We developed Magis as an

18-month program for lay people working in Jesuit-sponsored institutions. Participants attend four two-day seminars and a retreat, along with completing regular reading, personal reflection, and prayer. They come from all around the Maryland Province to take part in the program and find the experience enriching and transformative.

After that, the provincial invited Jesuits and lay colleagues to join in a Year of Prayer from October 2005 through May 2006. The Mission and Renewal team got together and produced a guidebook titled *Co-Laboring with the Living Lord: Ignatian Companions on Mission*, to be used during the year. The book, like the Spiritual Exercises themselves, aims at helping us to be open and disposed in mind and heart, to listen and respond generously to God: the One who is living in us and our history, laboring so that our world becomes, ever more so, the Kingdom of God on earth; the One who is calling out to us to be faithful co-laborers with God and one another. The Year was divided into four unfolding "Seasons," each disposing us to grow in a particular grace from the Lord: Gratitude, Healing, Call, and Co-Laboring. Brown said, "At the heart of this Year is our desire to deepen the roots of our companionship and refresh the Ignatian vision that inspires every one of the works of the Maryland Province—our educational institutions, our parishes, and our social and spiritual ministries."

In the wake of the Maryland Province Year of Prayer, I was contacted by Joseph P. Lacey, pastor of St. Alphonsus Rodriguez Church in Woodstock, Maryland. He asked me to meet with him and a few parishioners to plan a similar year of prayer for their Jesuit parish. After many meetings with the parish Ignatian Leadership Team (including with Dee Papania, a woman who is now leading a parish as a lay person), a manual for their year of prayer was complete and printed. Lacey explained to his parishioners in the introduction to the book, "The purpose of this year of prayer is well expressed on one of the final pages of this book in Father Pedro Arrupe's beautiful reflection on life. We pray through the Exercises quite simply in order that we may fall in love with Christ…" (*Our Parish Year of Prayer: Finding God in All Things as Companions of Jesus, Praying our Tradition and Mission*, St Alphonsus Rodriguez Church, October 2011—May 2012.)

At the time, I also heard from Ligouri Publications, requesting that I prepare a book for a series they were doing called "Lent and Easter Wisdom." I put together a selection of readings from St. Ignatius, illuminated by Scripture, along with my insights into Ignatian spirituality for the modern Christian. Each day provides the reader with words from St. Ignatius, a Scripture passage, a short reflection, and an action that aids the reader in discerning God's will in one's life. *Lent and Easter Wisdom from St. Ignatius of Loyola* was published in 2009.

Back at Loyola

While working in the provincial's office and living at the Loyola University Jesuit Community, the University Human Resources department asked me to speak regularly at new employee orientations about the Ignatian identity, mission, history, and core values of Loyola University.

I also had opportunities to meet with students at Loyola who were participating in a program called "Encounter El Salvador." It was a 10-day "faith-based immersion experience where participants learn from Salvadoran people about their lives, histories, and hopes for the future. A major focus of the encounter is to reflect on the meaning of working for justice rather than working for charity, understanding one's role as a global citizen and humanizing the different issues that are present in our societies," as described on Loyola University's website. We would meet before the students left to celebrate a liturgy. Then I would share my experiences at Archbishop (Saint) Oscar Romero's funeral. I would also tell them about the five Jesuits teaching at the University of Central America who were brutally killed in 1989 along with their housekeeper and her daughter, and share a homily that I gave at St. Ignatius Church in Baltimore on November 14, 2004, to commemorate the 15th anniversary of their deaths [which is presented as Chapter 31 in Part III of this volume].

In the homily, I spoke of how these martyrs had a "prophetic mission," which featured several dimensions—including an intellectual one. I pointed out that "all of the Jesuit martyrs were university professors who were amazingly well published, and whose research cut deep and exercised a profound influence on their ministry of prophetic proclamation. As scholars, they joined critical intelligence to passionate commitment—mind with heart—in service to the prophetic mission of the whole Church of El Salvador.

"And what of us?" I asked. "Is there a message here? I would suggest that, in their well-informed prophetic ministry, the Jesuit martyrs of El Salvador are issuing a call to us to 'go and do likewise.' As we look at our own current historical situation, what Word do we hear God uttering to us? Are we well enough informed to hear it accurately? And, if we are, have we got the prophetic courage to speak out—to act out—with the boldness of the Gospel?"

Whenever the Loyola University students returned from their immersion experience in El Salvador, we met again to reflect on their experiences.

At the Loyola University Sellinger School of Business, I collaborated with the school's dean, Karyl Leggio, to bring "the relevance of religious faith to business practice." We did so by hosting luncheon meetings in the Jesuit residence with business-school faculty members and by directing retreats for the faculty, all for the purpose of reflecting on Jesuit education, especially Jesuit business education. My work with the Sellinger School continued until Leggio stepped down as dean and returned to the classroom as a full-time Loyola finance professor in the fall of 2014. She continues to participate in our monthly meetings of the Baltimore chapter of the Woodstock Business Conference.

As noted earlier, the Woodstock Business Conference (WBC) is an initiative that started under the business ethics program when I was at Woodstock. It is a national program with chapters throughout the United States bringing business leaders together to discover the relevance of religious faith to business practice. Most of the monthly meetings are hosted by either higher education institutions or Catholic parish centers. As dean, Leggio had provided us with meeting space at the Sellinger school, and now the gatherings have moved to Colombiere Jesuit Community, where I now reside.

More recently, I collaborated with William J. Byron, S.J., on a book published by Paulist Press in 2016 and titled *Principles of Ignatian Leadership: A Resource for a Faith-Committed Life*. Bill and I have been lifelong friends—he is now a professor of business and society at St. Joseph's University in Philadelphia. We wanted to offer this book as a resource for men and women with leadership potential to internalize and apply Ignatian principles to their work and daily life—whether in a religious or completely secular setting

There are many succinct leadership lessons in the book, following quotes from Ignatius and other Jesuit sources. Here's one: "There is no substitute for good character in a leader. Love of the organization and its members is essential, as are magnanimity of spirit and generosity of heart. Prestige and good reputation are not to be disdained by a leader, just contained within humility." I believe these and other Ignatian principles are needed now more than ever, in a society thirsting for purpose and meaning—and servant leadership.

10.

A Jesuit Never Retires

Colombiere Jesuit Community, Baltimore, May 2016 to Present

In May of 2016, I moved to the St. Claude la Colombiere Jesuit Community, which was built for senior Jesuits to "age in place." Architecturally it is a beautiful, open, and serene environment. My room is spacious and comfortable with a beautiful view of rolling lawns and tall trees. The chapel is stunning and peaceful, and just a few steps from my room. We also have a library, exercise room, and other common areas, inside and out, so I am quite content here.

I feel like I've come full circle because the Colombiere Jesuit community sits on the ground where the provincial's office once stood at 5704 Roland Avenue.

It is often said that Jesuits never retire, and I want this saying to be very true for me. I think it has remained true, despite one, very big fact about my current existence: Shortly after moving into Colombiere, I was officially diagnosed with Alzheimer's disease, which affects one's memory as well as intelligence, imagination, and personality. I tell people these days—semi-seriously—"I don't DO proper nouns anymore!" It was because of my Alzheimer's, not yet diagnosed at the time, that I lost the privilege to drive a car and was sent from Loyola University to this community for so-called "retired" Jesuits.

Even with these limitations, I stay quite active academically, spiritually, and pastorally. For instance, every morning I develop an email to about 70 people (my "parishioners!")—a homily on the scriptural readings and the saint (if there is one) of the day. I also remain an active adviser and participant in the monthly meetings of the Woodstock

Business Conference's Baltimore group. And, I'm always available for counseling or advising others at their request.

Bill McFadden, my old Jesuit novitiate buddy and fellow songster, recently moved to the Colombiere Residence after many decades at Georgetown University. Who knows, we may put together another barbershop quartet. Stay tuned!

AMEN!

PART II

Reflection …

Homilies for Holy Trinity, 1982-1987

11.

Behind the Scenes, at the Incarnation

A Midnight Mass

On Christmas Day, we come to a manger. We come in excitement to gaze once again on the face of a baby. We come in wonder to look upon the human face and physical form in which God himself first entered human history.

Veiled in darkness from the beginning of creation, God has come today to reveal himself to us, to show us who he is, and to smile upon us with a human face. Today we learn (Luke 2:1-14) that the Almighty Creator of the Universe, the God of our Fathers Abraham, Isaac, and Jacob, is a God of LOVE. In a baby's face, we see the simplicity, the vulnerability, the playfulness, and the charm of God's love. No wonder we race in excitement to come again and enjoy the very first manifestation of God in all human history. For this baby calls forth our own love and affection.

As we gaze deeply into the eyes of that infant, we can feel ourselves drawn inward and downward to wonder over the "why" of that decision which brought this infant to birth. As we look at this plump and playful baby boy, we wonder why and what it is that God is revealing to us here. We contemplate the Divine Second Person of the Trinity, who reveals himself in a new way by fully and truly assuming our human nature.

In a wonderful meditation in his Spiritual Exercises, Saint Ignatius Loyola takes us in and through the eyes of this little baby, takes us "behind the scenes," as it were, to the motives of the Blessed Trinity in deciding that one of their number should take flesh and become a person.Saint Ignatius invites us to be a quiet observer in the company and the conversation of Father, Son, and Holy Spirit, as, from their heavenly vantage point, they gaze down upon our world in the time prior to the Incarnation. We, too, look down and see our earth with their eyes. And what we see with them, Ignatius tells us, is this: We see the whole expanse of all the earth, filled with human beings in the great diversity of human existence. Some are white, and some are black; some at peace, some at war; some weeping, and some laughing; some who are well, others who are sick; those coming into the world, those dying, and so on. We look down upon the whole surface of the earth and behold all nations in great blindness, swearing and blaspheming, wounding and killing, going down to death and descending into the hell they are creating.

Then, Ignatius invites us to feel and be moved with the heart of the Trinity. And the movement we feel with them, THEIR movement within our heart, is one of deep COMPASSION for such an afflicted world. Together with the Trinity, we feel that movement of compassion leading on to DECISION, the decision to send the Son, the Second Person of the Trinity, to become a person in order to save the human race.

This decision, deep in the heart of the Triune God, finds expression, then, in this little baby, the infant boy, lying in a manger, wrapped in swaddling clothes. He is a child of compassion. And it is this fire of love that radiates from his crib.

It is, as we know, a fire that will set the world ablaze, as this child grows to adulthood. "I have come to cast fire on the earth," Jesus will say.

It is the blaze of Trinitarian compassion, the flame of love, the bonfire of His Holy Spirit. And catch that fire did. First in the small band of his immediate disciples, and then, spreading through them into the hearts of others. Generation upon generation became kindled with the fire of Christ's love, passing the torch to succeeding generations, until that fire had spread to the ends of the earth.

And we, in our own time, have been touched by the compassion of God. We have been enkindled by the fire of His Spirit, and carry the torch of love and faith to yet another generation. We have become heirs in that mysterious and moving decision deep in the heart of the Trinity long ago, to save the human family from self-destruction. The challenge is now ours in a world still groaning for redemption.

So, it is with nostalgia, as well as love, that we return once again to this creche, this manger, this crib, and this child, to refresh ourselves and rekindle our hearts at this first flickering of divine love in our world. It is a homecoming for us—a return to our roots—as well as a birthday for Jesus.

Indeed, it IS a Merry Christmas!

12.
The Magi and Herod Inside Each of Us

Feast of the Epiphany

The last section to be written in any book, I am told, is the Introduction. That's because it is only in retrospect, after the story has been told, that we can (to shift the metaphor slightly) compose the overture of an opera, catching up and sounding the rich, dominant themes of what is to come.

And so it is with St. Matthew's Gospel. The last part to be composed was the first, the Infancy Narratives. It's an overture, richly elaborated usually in Old Testament imagery and introducing the major themes that will weave throughout the story to follow—from public life to Pentecost, and even beyond, including the early life of the Church itself.

Today's story of the Magi (Matthew 2:1-12) is one of the Infancy Narratives, the opening overture. Drawing on the prophecy of Isaiah, which we heard as our first reading today, it depicts in story form what the eyes of faith see happening when God-made-man becomes manifest to others. It tells us how humans can react to the Epiphany, that is, the appearance, of God in our world.

The reactions are two. The central figures, of course, are the magi. The sub-plot is Herod. Each play over-and-against and accentuates the other. The Magi search out Christ at great sacrifice in order to adore him. Herod searches out Christ at great sacrifice in order to destroy him.

The Magi are idealists, the stargazers of history, with the freedom to leave home on a journey they know not whither, simply because they feel called by a star to set out and go. Herod is a pragmatist, so captivated by the status quo—his position of power over his country folk—that he will do anything, including killing, to maintain it. St. Matthew consciously depicts him as the Egyptian Pharaoh of old who will slaughter a thousand innocents in order to eliminate one Moses. It is control at any cost.

The Magi are gentiles from a distant place, representing the far-flung world which St. Paul will visit, and which will embrace Christ and his Gospel with enthusiasm. Herod is a Jew and plays out that great paradox of history, namely, that many in Jesus' own land will reject him, and thereby and unwittingly propel the spread of his message and His Church throughout the world. (Isn't it strange how rejection produced propagation?)

So, in his story of the Magi and Herod, Matthew is telling us in broad, imaginative strokes about the paradox of Jesus: the focal point of both acceptance and rejection. He is a sign of contradiction, a two-edged sword, a cornerstone and a stumbling block. In his kindness, he comforts some—and outrages others. In his firmness, he consoles—and rebukes. In his fidelity and love, he inspires—and withers. It's all in the eye of the beholder. Magi or Herod.

And, of course, there is a Magi and a Herod inside each one of us. It's not simply across the pages of world history or through the course of centuries that this drama gets played out, as it certainly does. It gets played out also in the course of the personal history of each one of us. We know it in our own experience. With Herod and under the prompting of the Herod within us, we experience outrage at the unsettling demands of Christ's call to love, a life of generous service and self-sacrifice. How dare he erupt and intervene into the quiet and complacency of my life? How dare he force his Epiphany upon me? We can—and do—rue the day that God was born into this world of our consciousness. Why won't he let us be?

On the other hand, the Magi within us rejoices that this most human and loving of all persons has been revealed as our God, assuring us that nothing that is human, nothing of life or love, can be in vain, but is of supremely everlasting worth. As Magi, we collapse in tearful and grateful joy at the realization that, come what may, fail as we might, doubt as we will, the unfailing love of God will, indeed, raise us up to His own glory, the fullness of the freedom of the children of God.

It is the Herod and the Magi inside of us, then, which are pitted in contest. A contest unto death. But the end of the story is instructive. At the end of the story we know that Herod died. Of the Magi we learn no such thing. They go off, according to the story, apparently to "live happily ever after," as so many fairy tales end.

We know, just as convincingly, that it is the Magi in us who will "live happily ever after." That's God's promise, a promise that is rock-ribbed. And isn't that Good News?

13.

"Is this Mary's Boy?"

Jesus Grows Up Fast

Today is exactly one month and one day since Christmas. And already we find Jesus beginning his public life in this Gospel according to St. Luke.

Jesus grows up quickly in the Liturgical Year! Each year from Advent to Pentecost, we relive the whole of Christ's life with him so that we can be drawn more deeply into him in the annual reliving of the experience. We find him in his home town of Nazareth, having just returned from his baptism in the Jordan and his temptations in the desert. We see Jesus arriving at the synagogue of Nazareth, a synagogue he knew so well, with a congregation that had known him from infancy. The service begins and Jesus comes forward to do the reading. He is handed the Scripture of the day, a text from the prophet Isaiah. He reads:

> *The spirit of the Lord is upon me;*
> *because he has anointed me.*
> *He has sent me to bring glad tidings, the good news,*
> *to the poor;*
> *to proclaim liberty to captives,*
> *Recovery of sight to the blind,*
> *and release to prisoners.*

Then he rolls up the scroll, gives it back to the leader of the synagogue service, and says to the congregation, "Today this Scripture passage is fulfilled in your hearing."

That is the only quotation we have from his sermon (Luke 4:14-30). But it is really all we need to hear. Jesus said volumes in that short sentence about himself, about his Father, about his mission, and about the people in his congregation.

About himself he says that he is the prophet, because he has been specially anointed by God in some mysterious way and has been SENT by God to them and to the world. About his mission, he says that it is to bring good news to the poor, liberty to captives, sight to the blind, and release to prisoners. And about his congregation, he says: YOU are the poor, the captives, the blind, and the prisoners to whom I have been sent by God to bring joy, light, and freedom.

The congregation rejoices momentarily, proud of the eloquence and sincerity of this local boy. But in a moment the full impact of his message strikes home. We can almost hear them gasp, and then a murmur runs through the congregation. "Did I hear him correctly? Did he imply—did he say—that WE are the poor, and captives, and blind, and prisoners? Who does he think he is? Isn't this just Mary's boy, the son of the carpenter? We know him. How dare he?" And we're told that they tried to kill him by throwing him off the ledge of a hill on which the town was built. We'll read this sequel in next Sunday's Gospel, but today's story is not complete without it.

There is a deep message in this incident. It is this: Jesus cannot be the Good News, cannot be the Savior, cannot be the healer, and cannot be the redeemer or liberator of anyone who refuses to recognize and acknowledge that they NEED healing, freeing, and saving. And it says that that healing, freeing, and saving can only come to us from God through Jesus.

I cannot speak for you, but, personally, I vacillate in and out of that faith in God as my only healer and savior. And the vacillation depends on the degree to which I am conscious of my absolute need of Him for sight, integrity, and freedom. Sometimes I can fairly taste my desperate neediness and know experientially that only God can give me peace and wisdom and the self-possession we know as freedom. But, then, when things go smoothly, I'll forget that it all comes from Him and coast on it as though it were MINE or came from me. Then I lose it and become anxious, self-preoccupied, confused; and I find myself treating others as though they were my enemies instead of my brothers and sisters. I find that I am either fearing them or despising them, in those moments.

Eventually—thus far in my life—I have been reawakened to the misery of my plight, to my blindness and captivity, and returned like the Prodigal Son, throwing myself on God's mercy and His strength for me and in me. And peace returns.

Does this vacillating process sound at all familiar to you?

What this vacillating and cyclic experience says to me is this: my challenge is always to take special care to remember that God alone gives freedom, strength, light, and joy: to remember that these are His gifts and beyond my possession or manufacturing in myself. And to be grateful for these gifts when I experience them, never taking them for granted, lest I lose them and myself. What I can do, then, what WE can do, is always to dispose ourselves, hold ourselves in readiness, for the gifts of personhood which God alone can give.

So, the very first scene in the opening of Jesus' public life according to St. Luke, is itself, in telescoped form, the history of a lifetime—His and ours.

14.

Jesus the Partygoer

At a Wedding, in Cana

Today we celebrate the first of Jesus' miracles—turning water into wine, at the Wedding Feast at Cana (John 2:1-12). It is the next step in the unfolding story of his life and mission, which began at Christmas and will conclude in the Easter season.

It is interesting and instructive to relive this story in memory and imagination because Christ's life is the pattern of the unfolding and growth of our own lives. A rose can only unfold and grow as a rose, not a water buffalo. A lion must unfold and grow like a lion, not a daisy. We humans can only unfold and grow as Christ did, because he is THE human par excellence, the first among many brothers and sisters. His life is ours, and vice versa.

Well, what does the Wedding Feast of Cana tell us about the unfolding and growth of Jesus—and ourselves?

Of the many facets of this elaborate story, two seem especially interesting. First, Jesus is a partygoer. Second, He is there as one who serves.

Yes, Jesus is a partygoer. I dare say that if any of us had been commissioned to write the script for the first miracle of the Almighty God become man, we would hardly have set the scene at a party. God at a party? You've got to be kidding! I mean, the salvation of the whole human family from the clutches of evil is serious business. And the son of God has to appear serious about it. A party indeed!

Can you imagine John the Baptist at a party? Walking in wearing his camel's hair loin cloth and ordering a plate of locusts? Impossible. And what about Elijah, Moses, or Isaiah? Would they come to a party to deliver their stern mission of conversion? Not likely. They were clearly men of God, and men of God are not partygoers, right?

So, with his party going and wine bibbing, Jesus hardly seems to be earning his credentials as a prophet—let alone as Son of God. So we might think. And so thought the religious leaders of his day: the scribes, Pharisees, and high priests. "A drunkard," they called him. "A wine bibber," they said, and worse yet, "A friend of prostitutes and tax collectors." It was not at all what they expected from the hoped-for Messiah.

Well, it had long been said that "God's ways are not our ways." And it became quickly clear that Jesus' ways were not the ways of the scribes and Pharisees. It is clear that Jesus wanted to be with people—all the people—right where people are, in the everyday, ordinary events of their lives. He made it clear that he hadn't come all that distance just to stand apart from us, like some kind of living signpost pointing mutely to a purely spiritual way of salvation. What he made behaviorally clear was that he came to be ONE OF US in working out together with us the way for growing humanly toward the fulfillment of God's hopes and expectations for all of us.

Somewhere in the course of his growing up, Jesus had reached the conviction that we grow as humans in our relations with one another. We—each of us—grow in community, in our interactions with one another. And what is that place where human interaction is most open, relaxed, frequent, and susceptible of transformation? At parties, of course. So, to parties Jesus goes . . . to join with others in interaction. He learns and teaches, he influences and is influenced, he comes to know and be known, in the give and take of personal exchange.

The second facet of our story is that Jesus is there as one who serves. Notice that he is not just there to be entertained. He doesn't sit back as a spectator. He is very much involved as a contributor to the festivities. And, especially, when a need is brought to his attention—an absolutely desperate need as wedding parties go: wine—he is ready to respond. He does so generously, and tactfully.

His generosity is obvious. Biblical scholars figure that the water jars held about 120 gallons. No matter that the guests have already imbibed amply by this time. Jesus provides 120 gallons of the best wine the head steward has tasted. The party must go on.

And notice how tactfully he does it. None of the guests—not even the head steward—know where this wine has come from. Bride, groom, and guests don't even realize that the wine had run out. Only the servants immediately involved have any idea that a near-crisis was averted. Jesus' disciples and mother who were sitting with him, of course, also notice. But no one else.

Jesus does what needs doing and he does it without fanfare or personal attention to himself. What consideration for the bride and groom—those in embarrassing need—and for the guests! "I am among you as one who serves," Jesus once said of himself, and this story is a very good illustration of same.

And, of course, HE is growing in the process. It is through his selfless attentiveness to the needs of others that he grows in "wisdom, age, and grace." And if that's the way he grows, then, clearly, that's the way WE grow. We grow, not to be looking out for ourselves, but by discovering and responding to the needs of others. That's the way we grow together! It's the paradox of the Christian life: we grow by giving to others.

Finally, a concluding P.S.—in fairness to St. John's intention in writing this story. John clearly wants us to see this story as a PARABLE of things to come. By making this the first of Jesus' miracles, John wants us to think of the last great miracle of his life and ours. He wants us to see here an announcement and a foreshadowing of that great party to end all parties: the everlasting banquet in the Kingdom of Heaven.

What John underscores in his imagery of a wedding feast is both our challenge and our hope. Our hope is for a life eternal of banqueting together in joy, harmony, peace, and justice. Our challenge is to live right now as to dispose our human family for the magnificent transformation that will make it all come true. What we do daily—how we relate to one another here and now—has eternal significance for the banquet to be.

The invitation is out. The RSVPs are included. Can you make it?

15.

Let's Ask the Desert

Thoughts, on Ash Wednesday and the First Sunday of Lent

The forty days of Lent are patterned on the forty days which Jesus spent in the desert, immediately after his baptism by John in the Jordan and immediately prior to the beginning of his public ministry. He went into the desert to make a forty-day retreat, alone and in silence—there to wrestle with the demons of darkness and to find the light of God's guidance for his future. And struggle he did, as we know from the story of his temptations by Satan in St. Matthew's Gospel. Through three successively blatant temptations, Satan tried to make Jesus base his life and mission on the self-regarding motives of comfort, prestige, and power. He wanted Jesus to be self-serving. But Jesus' consistent and resounding reply was, "You shall worship the Lord your God and Him only shall you serve . . . . " And that became the standard and motto of his life and mission.
—From an Ash Wednesday homily

Four days later, on the First Sunday of Lent

I have a friend. And about this time last year, he found himself having second thoughts about a lot of important things in his life. He started wondering, for instance, whether he should quit his job—even though it was secure and well-paying—so he could do something more satisfying to himself and more helpful to others. He began to have serious, second thoughts about what he really believed in, about his values and lifestyle.

He seemed, in other words, to be at a fork in the road for some strange reason and he didn't quite know how to handle it.

Well, it was about that time that he learned of an interesting kind of retreat experience that some organization runs out West. So, he signed up and flew out to their central headquarters in California. He spent two days in an orientation session with about eight other people like himself. And then, each of them, separately, was flown by helicopter out into a desert where they were dropped off to spend the next four days all alone with nothing but the survival kits in the backpack they carried with them.

The idea is that you spend the four days all by yourself in the desert, just thinking and praying. He says it was quite an experience. Look in any direction, and all you see, stretching mile after mile, is sand and sky. No people, no buildings, no trees, no cars, nothing. And the only sound you hear is the breeze blowing over the sand and in your hair. No radios, TVs, music players, street noise, phones—nothing. No one to talk to and nothing to read. Just you, the desert, and the silence.

It's amazing, he says, how simple life gets right away. One of the first questions to come up, of course, is "Will I survive out here all by myself?" It becomes that fundamental, that fast. Then you start wondering how you will survive all alone. What will you do with yourself? And, finally, it is not long before you find yourself facing questions about the purpose or point of surviving at all. It's the "why" question. What does make life worth living? What's it for? What is "good"—and, on the flip side, what is evil?

He says it's really astounding how so many things that seemed so absolutely essential to your ordinary workaday life look trivial or very secondary when you're all alone in the desert. How you're dressed, what you look like, how you're impressing people, how much you earn or own—all these questions get parked in a back seat when you're in the desert. They look dumb when your attention is riveted on survival, life or death, and what difference it makes? The desert, my friend said, is a great place for sorting out sense from nonsense, essentials from trivia, truth from charade, good from evil, God's will from human sinfulness, decisions from deceptions.

Well, I thought of my friend's story immediately when I read the Gospel today (Mark 1:12-15), because it tells exactly the same story about

Jesus. He went out to the desert, like my friend, at a crossroads-time in his life in order to think and pray. Both found themselves getting right down to the important issues in life when they were uncluttered from the ordinary round of distraction and seductions. Listening to my friend's story helps me to understand better what it was like for Jesus.

It helped me especially to see why Satan's temptations fell on such deaf ears. Imagine it! Here is Jesus grappling in the desert with the really important life and death issues of survival and purpose, and up comes the Devil trying to tempt him with really second-rate seductions. *Do a little trick; turn stones into bread. Be a big shot, jump down off the top of the Temple and wow the crowd below, they'll really think you're important. Wouldn't it be great if you were the owner and the ruler of all the world; you'd be the big shot of the ages.* I can almost hear Jesus saying, "Are you trying to kid me? So, who's interested in doing slick tricks, making a big impression on people, or having wealth and power for a few years? I'm really not interested right now. I'm not interested in baubles and bangles, tricks and trivia, what people *think* I am or own. I'm interested in who I am and how I stand before God." Clearly, Satan picked the wrong guy in the wrong place. Jesus could see Satan's suggestions from his desert perspective and they didn't make sense at all.

Well, the Church has made the season of Lent forty days long, to remind us that we are invited to the same kind of desert experience that Jesus and my friend had. The Church invites us to do our best to unclutter our lives from distractions, so that we can see what's really important in our lives and what's trivial. It asks us to try to build a desert of quiet time for prayer and pondering, for reading and reflection. Prayer, fasting, and almsgiving are the traditional Lenten practices because they remind us that noise and splash, food and money can become possessive of us, rather than the other way around.

Let's try to head for the desert in imagination and see how things look to us when we're out there. What's important and what takes a back seat? What do we really want to do? Let's ask the desert.

16.
Christ's Transfiguration, and Ours
Turning from Fear of Life to the Glow of Joy

…. [Jesus] took Peter, John, and James and went up the mountain to pray. While he was praying his face changed in appearance and his clothing became dazzling white. And behold, two men were conversing with him, Moses and Elijah, who appeared in glory and spoke of his exodus that he was going to accomplish in Jerusalem. Peter and his companions had been overcome by sleep, but becoming fully awake, they saw his glory….
—Luke 9:28-32

It is quite a striking, even bedazzling, story—the Transfiguration of Jesus, in St. Luke's Gospel. The imagery is rich, the scene glows with radiance and magnificence, as the evangelist struggles to depict a transformation in Jesus' feelings and person, as he sets his face toward his passion, death, and resurrection in Jerusalem.

Though perhaps not as profound or dazzling as this scene, we all have had some experience of transfiguration or transformation in our own lives—enough, at any rate, to give us some inkling into the internal experience of Jesus in this incident.

For instance, I'll never forget watching my own father when he first saw his first grandchild. I was about 30 at the time, so I guess my father couldn't have been more than 65 or 66. To me he was an old man: double-chinned, loose-jowled, furrowed of forehead, and sagging of waistline. Rather a sourpuss, actually. My own mother used to call him the "terrible-tempered Mr. Bangs!" You've got the picture. Well, when he laid eyes on his first grandchild, I was simply astounded to see him turn into a child, himself, before my very eyes. His eyes danced with wonder and delight. His mouth was wreathed in a smile of unselfconscious merriment. His whole face softened and glowed before the miracle of new birth—and of his own flesh and blood. He looked like a four-year-old at Christmas, oohing and cooing!

THAT was a transfiguration, a transformation of personality. And it wasn't just physical; it was deeply and interiorly personal. He had been touched and enlightened in his very BEING.

We've all had experiences like that in our lives. I could describe a dozen others, and so could you. So, we're no strangers to transfiguration. We've seen people come alive in a whole new way because they have been touched with a new insight, a new joy, and a new gift. So, we have SOME, even if partial, experience of what Christ's Transfiguration might have been like.

But what is it that so transforms Jesus' experience, inside and out? What sets him aglow? What is it that has picked him up, raised him up, exalted him to such radiance?

St. Luke lets us know by relating what Jesus was talking about with Moses and Elijah. Here's what Luke says: "Moses and Elijah … were talking to Jesus about the passage he was about to complete in Jerusalem." It is the expectation of the completion of his passage that so thrills and transforms Jesus. His passage-completed rejoices him.

That word "passage" is a very ancient one for Luke and a very familiar one to us. You'll recognize it immediately when I tell you that Luke's Greek word for "passage" is "EXODUS." It is the word used to describe the departure of the ancient Israelites from Egypt under the oppressive domination of the Pharaoh, as well as their 40-year journey through the desert to the Promised Land. That is the ancient EXODUS. That was their passage. And it came also to be called their PASSOVER, which they celebrated in feast ever after—to our own day. It is a celebration of passage from slavery to freedom, from alienation to homecoming, from grinding and humiliating despotism under the Pharaoh to the kindly and supportive love of God. It was—and they KNEW it was—ALL GOD'S doing for them. It was by his power that they escaped and resettled. They were overwhelmed by the appreciation that, of all the peoples on earth, God had chosen THEM for his special care, that He had chosen THEM to be His special people and lead them to such a special land, flowing with milk and honey. Their joy was transfiguring.

It is in this same imagery, then, that Jesus conceives his own experience, at that moment of transfiguration and the days to come. He sees his journey to Jerusalem, he sees his arrest, his trial, his condemnation, his crucifixion, and his death—he sees all of it as the emancipation that God is working within him. Caught at this moment in the worldly webs of hostility, humiliation, and oppression, he looks forward to that great day—soon, now, to come—when he will pass out of this world and into the home of his loving Father. By standing steadfastly to his own LOVE—love for God and love for humankind—Jesus will experience his death as a Passover to the most unbelievable peace possible, to the joy in the loving presence of His Father, to a freedom he has never yet known as man.

No wonder, then, that Jesus glows at the expectation of the completion of his passage. His confident hope, his longing to be fulfilled, his assurance in the Father's fidelity to his promise, will all sustain him in peace in the midst of the worst torment that his enemies can perpetrate on him. He can suffer life's worst, because his eyes are set on both his final, earthly mission and life everlasting.

Let's ask God to reinvigorate our own HOPE this Lent. Let's ask him to raise our eyes and hearts to the Kingdom which is to come. Let's pray for a transfiguration of ourselves from fear of life and the monotony of routine to a glow of joy in what is yet to come.

17.

Whodunit?

An Easter Homily

Our Gospel on this great celebration of Easter reads like a mystery novel—a *whodunit*. It tells of a strange event with all the earmarks of a crime. At least, that's what Mary Magdalene immediately concluded.

In John 20:1-9, we hear how she went early in the morning to the tomb in which they'd buried Jesus. Discovering that the huge stone has been rolled away from the entrance, she concludes that someone has broken in and stolen Jesus' body. That's the report, at any rate, which she delivers breathlessly to Peter and John, once she's tracked them down.

Her strange story moves the two disciples to immediate action. They head straight for the tomb—not walking, but running. It's interesting that young John outraces Peter. Perhaps it's youth that gives his step that extra spring. Or maybe it's something else. We'll see.

At any rate, arriving at the tomb, they, too, see the displaced boulder. But emboldened by their companionship, they go right into the little cave. All they find are the long strips of cloth in which Jesus' body had been wrapped. His body-wrapping is disheveled in a lump on the floor, while the wrapping on his face is neatly folded and placed apart by itself. Very strange. These are clues, of course, but what do they point to? What has happened? Is it evidence of a theft? Or is there some other explanation?

Peter is frankly stumped. That much the story tells us.

It's John, we're told, who quickly diagnoses the clues and gets to the heart of the matter. He immediately discounts the possibility of theft. "Why in the world," he reasons more or less, "would a thief stop to strip the body naked before carrying it off? Why would thieves take the time and have the patience to fold up the head-wrapping so neatly, when they would be anxious to get away quickly and undetected? No, it doesn't make any sense!"

But, if not theft, then what is the alternative? John leaps with insight and conviction to what HAS to be the truth of the matter. It is that, somehow, it was Jesus himself who removed these wrappings from himself and, with characteristic patience, had folded up his face-wrapping before shoving back the stone and walking out to freedom. John looked at the clues and, as he admits, "We saw and believed." He believed that Jesus had risen from the dead. Astounding!

But why was John the one who came to this immediate intuition, just as it was John who outraced Peter to the tomb? In this question is a central message of the Gospel reading, and the answer is also in the story. We are told that John is "the disciple whom Jesus loved," and, by implication, John is the disciple who has special love and affection for Jesus. The clear message is that John's feet and heart are propelled by love—love for Jesus, and it is this love that enables John to read clues and interpret signs with the sensitivity and intuition that others lack. He sees with the eyes of a lover.

And standing in that Easter tomb, what John sees in a flash of insight is the full meaning of Good Friday. The pieces of that drama begin to tumble together in his head, and he recalls clearly how Jesus had not been the passive victim of others' atrocities. No, he had GIVEN his own life freely and lovingly for others. He realizes that Jesus had not been vanquished; his spirit had not been broken; his love had not been quenched. Death had no more conquered Jesus than these wrappings could hold him captive, or that huge stone imprison him. Trusting in God for his life, the power of God's love had sustained his life and transformed his existence. Love had conquered death, and Jesus lives.

All of this John, the lover, saw about Jesus, and believed. But, more than that, he also experienced a foretaste of resurrection for himself. For if death was not the final word for Jesus, then death could not be the final word for John. If the power of God's love raised Jesus from the dead, that same power could and would raise him to join the Jesus to whom he was linked in love. With ecstatic joy, he realized that NOTHING in life or death—suffering or persecution, fear or humiliation—could separate him from the life-sustaining love of God for him in Christ Jesus. And in that realization, he himself was transformed to a man free, joyous, and alive with the new life of Christ. The risen Christ raised John! The resurrection is in *us*.

And so, we believe. And so, we rejoice this Easter, as, with John, we look around our own tomb of earthly existence—a tomb that would purport to hold us captive through fear of death or the bondage of sin. We look around our tomb and realize joyfully that the stone HAS been rolled back and that we, too, will be led one day out that doorway which Christ has opened—to eternal life. "This is the day the Lord has made; let us rejoice and be glad." Happy Easter!

And Why Jesus Doesn't Pop Up More Often

From Another Easter Sermon

Why doesn't Jesus appear to us individually and visibly? He's got his own reasons, I'm sure, but I suspect one of them is that he doesn't want to distract us from what's really central to his mission and what he desires of us. (See Matthew 25, on that.) Jesus wants us to see him embodied in each of *us*. What he wanted from the beginning is that we love one another as he loves us.

And Jesus was divinized, so we are all divinized in him. And he wants us to love, respect, and cherish that dignity, the divine dignity, in each other. And thereby we build up the full body of Christ, the Kingdom of God in this world of ours, now and forever. *Amen.*

18.
The Craziness of Pentecost

Giving Away Love, Peace, and Freedom—Free of Charge

When I was a little boy, I met a man on my way home from school one day. He said to me, "How would you like to become rich?" I thought that would be just fine, and I told him so. Though I was only eight years old, I had long since become sick of being totally dependent on my mother and father.

So, "Fine," I say to the man, "I'd like to be rich. What do I do to get rich?"

"It's simple," he says. "I deliver you a whole bunch of magazines for a minimal cost, and you turn around and sell them one by one at a much bigger price. It's gravy. All the profit is yours. And your business is sure to boom once people see what a wonderful product you're selling."

"That's great," I say.

Well, a few days later the whole family is sitting at the dinner table when there is a knock at the back door, and there is the man with a whole bunch of magazines asking for me. I'm starting on my way out to see him when my father asks, "What's going on?" I tell him the whole wonderful story and how I'm sure to get very rich in no time at all. His reaction is not one of warm support. "Tell the guy to go away," he says. "But I've got an agreement with him," I tell my father. "You're a minor," he says, "nothing's binding."

After I broke my contract with my supplier, my father sat me down and gave me a long speech about business. We reflected together on this most recent micro-model of supply and demand (or lack thereof), of middle people and markups, of sound investing, and being conned. "With it all," my father wound it up, "this experience has taught you something;

it taught you what makes the world go 'round: the supply of goods and services at a price that makes you a profit. It's your PROFIT—YOUR bottom line—that drives the system. MAKING is your motivation."

I've often thought about that incident in the years since. I think I would have enjoyed being a business person. People have told me I'd make a terrific salesman. I could really get fueled up and motivated by making a profit. If that man with magazines came up to me again with the promise to make me rich, I might just bite all over again.

I say this because in my business everything is completely the opposite of that. Jesus came along one day and gave me a speech that is absolutely inside-out and upside-down of the speech the magazine pusher gave me. Jesus says, "I have something to GIVE you, free of charge and at no cost. It is yours for the asking—no, even BEFORE and without the asking. And what I'm proposing to you is that you go along and give this thing away to others—just pass it along to them free of charge and at no cost. I give it to you; you give it to them; and tell them to pass it on to someone else free of charge."

"What's in it for me?" I find myself asking Jesus.

"That's the wrong question," Jesus says. "The bottom line in my business is not what you've been able to get out of it, but how much you've been able to give out."

"What are you giving?" I ask Jesus.

"I'm giving FRIENDSHIP," he says. "I'm giving God's love, because to love me is to love the Father. Of course, knowing my love will make you feel freedom, and peace, and self-confidence, but that's not WHY you look for friendship. The profit motive mocks friendship, and kills it."

As I play out the script of this conversation in my head, I can't help but think how crazy it is. Give something for *nothing*? Give MYSELF, no less? And being told that this is the secret of life? I mean not just the bottom line of business, but the bottom line of being.

Well, that's the craziness of Pentecost. Read the Gospel (John 20:19-23): Jesus freely breathing his own life into his friends, so that they can rush out to breathe that life of love and friendship, forgiving, and understanding, into others. And off they ran and that's what they did. They did it very well. Friendship—Christian fellowship—has come on down the ages to this very day. We can look around and see ourselves surrounded by Christian friends—not a single one of whom came here today in the hope of personal profit. I haven't heard anyone say yet today: "What's in it for me?"

Isn't that crazy? What's wrong with them? What's wrong with us? But that's Pentecost for you. That's the craziness. That's the bottom line. Don't you think so, Dad?

19.

Why We Sing at Mass

We're not an Audience. We're Participants.

I have a confession to make. I'm an old *barbershopper*. You know what a Barbershop quartette is: four guys in ice-cream parlor jackets, wearing straw skimmers, and singing "Sweet Adeline" to the accompaniment of every alley cat in the neighborhood. I did it for years.

And one thing did come out of this experience. I learned the meaning of "interdependence in the human community" long before I'd heard of that mouthful of an expression. I mean, how could you be harmonizing with three other guys when one of us was hitting a bad note. WE NEEDED EACH OTHER. None of us sounded any good unless all of us sounded good. And when we were on, we were like one person. When we really hit it, we just glowed at each other with smiles of appreciation as broad as the ocean. Soul brothers we were.

So, I can understand why they talk about heaven as the "celestial choir." It's the perfect image—for an old *barbershopper*. It's the perfect image of harmony, peace, unity, and joy. Jesus might have said, "Repent! The Kingdom of God is at hand" (Mark 1:12-15). But I know that what he meant was, "I want to teach the world to sing in perfect harmony." If you think about it, it all comes down to the same thing, doesn't it?

And if the Mass is supposed to be a foretaste of heaven—all God's children gathered at His Banquet Table to celebrate their life together in him—then it makes all the sense in the world that we sing together. We simply HAVE to sing in our celebration of life. In singing we say who we are, and we become who we are: brothers and sisters in harmony. All for the praise and glory of God.

It's not surprising, then, that there's always been singing at Mass. It dates all the way back to the Last Supper, where Jesus and the apostles sang Psalms together in the course of their Passover meal. Psalms are songs, written to be accompanied by a kind of harp that is the great-great-granddaddy of the modern guitar.

* * *

After Christ's resurrection when the Church began to grow and spread to the East and the West, songs continued to be sung at Mass, in different languages (Hebrew, Greek, Latin), and in different styles and rhythms, according to the tastes and traditions of the different countries to which the Church spread.

A kind of golden era in Church singing was born somewhere around the year 600 with the invention of what we call "Gregorian Chant." This style of singing was popular for almost a thousand years. It was named after Pope Gregory I, who is famous for streamlining and reorganizing the Mass in his day. He died in 604. We still have Gregorian chants written in the 800s.

Gregorian is sung without accompaniment. It has only a melody line, no harmony. It is set to Latin Mass texts. It has a tricky rhythm of upbeat and downbeat, and gets its variety from quick changes, loud to soft. It has to flow like a brook and be light as a soufflé. It's a small sound, in a way, which is both sober and spirited.

Thanks to our *schola cantus* we're hearing it today. It's a trip down memory lane, as we listen and sing along with these "Golden Oldies" of Church music. It's back in touch with our roots.

But about the 17th century, Gregorian got moved off the center stage of Church music by a whole new sound. People discovered harmony for voices and also invented a variety of new musical instruments. And they found the combination very pleasing and much more to their liking. Great musical composers came along, like Bach and Beethoven, Mozart and Mahler, Palestrina and Verdi, and they made big, complicated, rich sounds of orchestra and church choir. A whole new era of Church music was ushered in.

In some ways this new music was a big advance over Gregorian Chant, but its performance in Church unconsciously tended to over-look the most important thing of all, namely, that music and singing are the community's way of joining together as one and of praising God. What happened was that the Church turned into a concert hall and the community had turned into an audience at a performance. The music was beautiful, but the community got bypassed because the music was un-singable by the community.

Back in 1965, Vatican II reminded us once again that the community or assembly is primary at Mass. We're not spectators; we are the performers. We're not here to be entertained; we're here to participate. We're not listeners; we're singers. Now, that was clear in the days of Gregorian Chant. And as we sing that Chant today, we are reminded again of our age-old identity as a singing community.

Gregorian probably won't catch on again as the meat and potatoes of our musical diet. Modern Church music is in transition as we look to discover and work to invent good music which is also singable. Our 9:30 music group has done a wonderful job, and they are still working at it for us. And God knows the 9:30 community has done a great job.

One visitor here recently actually wrote a letter of complaint to the archbishop that we sing LUSTILY. Actually, I was proud of that. Someone else said we sing so loud it sounds like a Protestant Church. I like that too. Let's continue to sing out, growing together, as we praise the Lord, in perfect harmony.

Jesuit Novice Jim Connor (second row, second from left)

May and Martin Connor visit their son at Wernersville

Working the grounds at Wernersville

Walking the grounds at Wernersville

Studying at the Gregorian and enjoying a visit from his father

A young priest with his family: father, mother, sister Mary Jane
and husband Bill, brother Marty and wife Ruth,
nephews, and nieces.

Maryland Provincial Jim Connor with Father General Pedro Arrupe
and New York Provincial Robert A. "Bob" Mitchell

Father Connor with Horace McKenna, S.J., March 17, 1982

Greeting Holy Trinity parishioners after Sunday Mass

Social Concerns Committee retreat at Manresa Retreat House:
Grace O'Connor, Father Connor, and Jim Nolan.

Inspecting windows with Fred Farmer, facilities director, Holy Trinity

Trinity Sunday Mass and annual parish picnic on the grounds
of Georgetown Visitation Convent

Father Connor in his Holy Trinity office in May 1987.
Behind him hangs a patchwork quilt made by parishioners
with each square representing a parish group.

Celebrating 50 years a Jesuit with Monsignor Richard Liddy, Woodstock
visiting fellow, and Joseph Tylenda, S.J., director of the Woodstock Library
September 29, 1996

Brother Marty and sister Mary Jane with Father Connor at the
Woodstock residence for the 50th anniversary dinner

Father Connor with Beth Kostelac, co-laborer at Woodstock
and Holy Trinity, at the anniversary dinner

Father Connor and Walter Burghardt, S.J., senior fellow,
Woodstock Theological Center, June 2000

Father Connor in the Colombiere House Chapel
on his 89th birthday, May 21, 2018

20.

A Spirituality for All

The Feast of St. Ignatius Loyola

Today, July 31, is the Feast of St. Ignatius Loyola (the Gospel reading is Luke 14:25-33). St. Ignatius was born in 1491 and is best remembered for having founded the Society of Jesus, whose members are popularly known as Jesuits. This is also a special feast for Holy Trinity parish because from its beginning in 1787, it is Jesuits who have staffed this first Catholic Church in Washington, D.C.

Right from its founding in 1540, the Society of Jesus provoked controversy because it broke radically from the traditional form of religious-order life in the Church. The most obvious difference was Ignatius' insistence that his men not be centered in a monastery but should go out and work actively with others in the world. And their lifestyle should be as flexible as this apostolic mobility required.

Unlike Benedictines, they would not live in a fixed monastery with regular hours for the divine office for prayer, rising and retiring, and the like. Unlike the Franciscans, they would have no identifiable dress or religious habit. Unlike the Dominicans, they would not have any distinguishing apostolic work, like preaching. They were not even to be bound in their mobility by diocesan territorial lines or be under the jurisdictional authority of local bishops. Rather, they would relate directly to the pope himself and be available to do any kind of work, anywhere in the world, wherever there was greatest need or hope of greater good.

Such a thing was unheard of for religious orders in the 16th century. And the proposal understandably met with astonishment and skepticism. "How," critics asked, "can this religious order be anything but disorganized, undisciplined and thoroughly dissipated, given the breadth of its ambitions and its freedom of lifestyle?" One cardinal said:

"Unless they stay home and chant the divine office, they will become dirty as Church mice!" Lacking the buttress of external identification, how can this group possibly have identity!

Grounds for these fears were certainly realistic. Ignatius himself was well aware of the risk he was taking. Nonetheless, he was absolutely adamant, in the face of great pressure from high places, that it could be done and that, given the state of the world, it needed to be done. He was convinced that unity, purpose, and identity could be sustained without reliance on the traditional externals of religious life.

But how? What did he have in mind? The search for an answer takes us back to the life experience of Ignatius himself.

Ignatius started adulthood, on his own admission, as an ambitious, vain, empty-headed, and worldly courtier and soldier. At the battle of Pamplona, he was severely wounded and faced a long, painful convalescence. In his boredom he asked for his favorite novels of courtly chivalry, knighthood, and romance. None were found in the Castle of Loyola where he was staying, so instead he was given a book on the life of Christ and another on the lives of the saints. At first, he only read the books to pass the time away but then he began to notice that when he read about the life of Christ or the lives of the saints, he would feel himself unexplainably drawn to admiration, a sense of purposefulness, and peace. But he would resist these feelings. Then he would remember that when he read about chivalry and romance, he would first find his ambitions flamed, but would subsequently experience hollowness, distaste, and restlessness. He would think of his feelings alternately and realized that knightly chivalry invariably left him restless and discontented in the end. The life of Christ and the lives of the saints left him strangely at peace.

Through long months of prayer and reflection, Ignatius proceeded to analyze this strange phenomenon. He began to realize that his worldly ambitions and sentimental romances were really putting him into a kind of personal imprisonment. They were poisoning his system, making him feel interiorly nauseous no matter how attractive they originally appeared. The life of Christ, on the other hand, had a liberating effect on him. The prospect of selfless service of others in the model of Christ brought him to an experience of freedom and rightness and peace that he had never before known. This, he came to see, was indeed the effect of God's work within him.

So out of his experience, Ignatius came up with three bedrock principles or truths:

First, God himself is personally present in the consciousness of each one of us and is active there, influencing our feelings without overriding our freedom.

Second, with self-discipline and God's grace, we can actually recognize certain feelings as invitations from God, leading us to discern where he wants us to go and what to do. Ignatius calls this the "discernment of spirits." By such discernment we learn God's will for us.

Third, to embrace and follow God's will, as so revealed within us, is the heart and soul, sum and substance, of the Christian life. It is all that God wants of us, for our own best good. As Dante had said, "In God's will is our peace." And to God's will, Ignatius devoted his entire life.

Eventually, Ignatius codified his spiritual experiences in a little book titled *The Spiritual Exercises*. It is a plan for a retreat lasting 30 days and follows the pattern of Ignatius' own spiritual pilgrimage. Every Jesuit who has ever lived has made the 30-day retreat of the Spiritual Exercises at least twice in his lifetime. Whether a Jesuit is American, or Indian, or African, or Asian, or whatever, he has been formed in the methodology of the Spiritual Exercises.

So, now, finally, we come back to our original question: What is the identity of the Society of Jesus? It is not in externals; it is rather in a distinctiveness of personality formed to the image of Christ in the pattern of the Ignatian experience. The unity of the Society of Jesus is rooted, finally, in the search for and following out of God's will according to the distinctive process, methodology, or spirituality of St. Ignatius.

This spirituality, which is available to all and not solely to Jesuits, is St. Ignatius' principal gift to the Church. The price he paid to leave us this heritage was his own personal sacrifice and persistent dedication to God's will. For this we are deeply grateful. And today, on his feast, we honor and thank him.

21.
Transcending "Us" and "Them"

What Jesus Learned from a Canaanite Woman

I knew a man who used to say that the world is divided into two parts: those who play the trombone and those who don't. He played the trombone and the distinction gave him the satisfaction of identifying who is "us" and who is "them." The same penchant for clear and distinct divisions underlay the remark of a famous Jesuit of days gone by who used to say, "All the Jesuits on the Eastern seaboard are divided into two groups: those who ARE stationed at Georgetown University and those who want to be!" As you might guess, he was stationed at Georgetown.

It is this penchant for dividing people into "them" and "us" that underlies the readings today. Who is in and who is out? Who fits and who doesn't? Who's "us" and who's "them."

In the first reading, Isaiah is addressing the situation in Israel after the Jewish people have come back to their homeland after years of exile in Babylon. They find the place now populated by pagans and gentiles. What are they to do? How are they to maintain their national unity and religious purity when these foreigners are intermingled with them? In an earlier tradition, propounded by Ezekiel, the pagan foreigners were to be driven out of the country even by force, if necessary, lest religion and culture be diluted and dissolved. But Isaiah takes another tack. It is a developmental step forward in Israel's theological self-understanding. Isaiah says that the foreigners may stay, on condition that they embrace the Jewish religion: by loving and serving the Lord, keeping the Covenant, and observing the Sabbath. Isaiah is saying a startling new thing here, namely, the Covenant is not only for those born and bred Jews by blood line, but is for all people who choose to embrace it. People can become Jews by "adoption," as it were. They can become "us," by free choice and personal commitment.

A similar situation is confronted in today's Gospel reading (Matthew 15:21-28). It is another case of who is "us" and who are "them?" Who can be "in" and who is clearly "out?" In this case, it has to do with Christianity and the Gospel Jesus has come to preach. And the question is: Is Jesus' message and saving action only for those who have first professed the Jewish religion, or is it open and available to non-Jews as well? It is a question that will not be fully answered until some years after Jesus' death, at the Council of Jerusalem described in Acts 15. But the seeds of that answer are already sown in Jesus' own life, as in the incident described today.

A Canaanite woman approaches Jesus asking him to cure her daughter. Now because of their behavior over a long history, the Canaanites were regarded by the Jews as such a wicked, sinful, and godless race that their expulsion was not only permitted but commended. So how can Jesus have anything to do with a Canaanite woman? And, indeed, as the story unfolds, it looks very much like he will have nothing to do with her. "It is not right to take the food of sons and daughters and throw it to dogs," he says to her—in one of the most insulting statements in the New Testament. It was undoubtedly softer to the ear within the rough-and-tumble context of earlier times, but it still carried a surprising sting.

Undaunted, the determined woman fires back her own clever but sincere rejoinder: "Please, Lord, even the dogs eat the leavings that fall from their masters' tables." Jesus is astounded. In fact, he's learned something. It's with genuine amazement that he says with a shake of the head, "Woman, you have great faith!" And by deciding to cure her daughter—which he did immediately—he has made a much more far-reaching decision: a decision about who is "in" and who is "out" in regard to his saving activity, his Gospel of salvation, and Christianity as a whole.

As will be made absolutely clear at the Council of Jerusalem, Jesus sees and decides that Christianity is truly catholic with a small "c." That is, its saving message is for all, about all, and in service to all regardless of race, sex, social status, nationality, or any other human division that establishes a "we" from a "them." It transcends all distinctions by laying bare our deepest, common ground of unity: the one God and Father of us all; Jesus, the one Lord of us all, and of history, too; the one Spirit who dissolves barriers as it draws us together in love; and our fundamental *familyhood* as human beings. All of us children at heart—brothers and sisters to one another.

As St. Paul says, "In Christ, there is no Jew or Gentile, slave or freedman, male or female." Beyond these distinctions we know our unity, because each of us know—really—who we are most fundamentally. And we confess this, every time we say the "Our Father" or the "Apostles' Creed."

This "who we really are" is the basic truth we are called to live out as Christians. It's as simple as that. In so living we grow in freedom, in unity, in peace, and the joy which stems from hope for what will be. But—and this is important—we Christians also live it out for the benefit of all other people, Christian or not. We recognize our own lives as witnesses for others to the truth which is true of them as well. Whatever they become, Christians or not—and many complex factors invariably enter into such a decision—we want others to know by our treatment of them that they, too, are our brothers and sisters, because they, too, are children of the same Father.

This, then, is the message of today's readings: Christianity is not sectarian; it is not a tribal cult; it is not the possession of a certain elite. To our Father and His Christ, there is no "us" and "them."

22.
Getting into Banqueting

Why the Kingdom of God is like a Rollicking Wedding Feast

When you are invited by someone to a wedding banquet, do not recline at table in the place of honor…. Rather, when you are invited, go and take the lowest place so that when the host comes to you he may say, "My friend, move up to a higher position." Then you will enjoy the esteem of your companions at the table.
For everyone who exalts himself will be humbled, but the one who humbles himself will be exalted.
—Luke 14:8-11

What Jesus is teaching us in today's Gospel is good table manners and how to behave ourselves at a banquet. It reminds me of the last thing my mother said to me the day I entered the Jesuit novitiate 40 years ago last month. Just before the iron gate swung shut between us, she said, "For heaven's sake, don't disgrace me with your table manners!" True story, I swear.

Jesus' motivation was a mite more refined than my mother's, but his message is basically the same. It's about those table manners and the way we behave at a banquet. He has some advice for the guests and also for the host. To the guests, he says, "For heaven's sake don't parade pompously up to the front seats and play the showoff to impress people. That's gross," Jesus says. "Definitely bad form." And to the host, Jesus says, "Don't manipulate people by pretending to be nice to them, when the real reason you've invited them to your party is to get something from them. Oink, oink; that's piggy," Jesus is saying. "Not good table manners at all."

115

The reason Jesus is so concerned about our table manners is that he expects we're going to spend an awful lot of time at a banquet. In fact, he expects we're going to spend all eternity at a very special banquet called the wedding feast of heaven. That's the way Scripture often describes heaven: as a wonderful, rollicking, happy wedding feast—eating and drinking and singing and laughing, and having a great old time.

But the thing is: Unless we're getting into banqueting now, we won't get into the banquet later on. You've got to be into it or you're just not into it. Does that sound crazy? Well, it's not; it's true. It's true for lots of things, not just heavenly banqueting.

Take certain kinds of music, for example. Either you're into it or you're not. If you're not into it, it means nothing to you. It sounds like rubbish, noise, bedlam. You probably think I'm talking about acid rock. I could be. But it's even true of opera or symphony. I remember years ago us kids asking our father to take us to an opera with him. He was a music buff—opera and symphony. We wanted to go, I think, just because he did. We didn't know music worth beans. In fact, we hated opera. Well, he said to us, "I'm not going to waste money on you kids unless you really know the opera." He told us that "La Boheme" by Puccini was coming in a month and he would take only the ones who could prove they really knew the music. We listened to "La Boheme" every afternoon for a month. I mean, we got INTO it. We got into opera. And it got into us. It was like a whole new world opened up and we walked in.

Swimming is another good example. My brother and I were sent to summer camp when we were kids. But when we got there we weren't allowed to swim with the other kids in the deep water until we had proven to the counsellors that we could swim in the shallow cove. "You can't swim unless you can swim," we were told, and that didn't sound like gobbledygook to us. We knew exactly what that meant. So, in the course of a week or two, we learned to swim, and then we could swim. You can't swim unless you are a swimmer.

Well, the same thing is true of heavenly banqueting. You simply can't banquet unless you're a banqueter—unless you know how to banquet. If you're not into it, it's a closed world for you. If you're outside—well, that's what the Scriptures mean about the gates of heaven being closed to some people. They're just not INTO it. They're OUT of it.

In the Gospel today, Jesus is saying, "Get into heavenly banqueting so that you can get into the heavenly banquet." In his parables, Jesus says that heavenly banqueting is not using other people either as an audience for my showing off or as a way to make me a profit. No, heavenly banqueting is sitting back and caring about other people getting ahead and doing well. It's being together and meshing well. Living like really good brothers and sisters—that's what this banqueting's all about.

So, let's get into banqueting right now, so we'll be into it when that great wedding feast comes breaking in from God knows where. And when heaven dawns, there we'll be—having a ball. It's going to be wonderful. Let's get into it.

23.

The Renunciation

"Sell All You Have!"

The sentence that jumped out at me when I first read today's Gospel (Luke 14:25-33) is the final sentence we just heard. It says, "In the same way, none of you can be my disciple unless you renounce all your possessions." With that sentence, Jesus gives the practical application of the stories he has just told, stories about people who need to calculate accurately before building towers or waging wars. Jesus seems to be saying that if we fail to calculate the renunciation of possessions into our decision to become a disciple, we are doomed to failure at the outset.

In fact, this is exactly what DOES happen to a young man just a few chapters later in St. Luke's Gospel. That will be in chapter 18 (:22). A young man will come up to Jesus and ask him, "What must I do, Lord, to possess eternal life?" Jesus tells him to keep the commandments, the Ten Commandments—as a good Jewish boy should. "I have done all these things since my youth," the young man says. "Then one thing only is lacking," Jesus answers. "Go, sell all you have and give it to the poor, and then come, follow me." We are told that the young man's face fell in sadness, and he walked away, because, the text says, "he was *very* wealthy." (In the Greek, *en gar plousios sphodra*—exceedingly.)

This theme of renunciation of wealth for the following of Jesus is central to the Gospel, especially in Luke. We tend to think of it as a hard saying. It causes us some nervousness and guilt, because it sounds so negative and repressive. In commending renunciation, however, Jesus is really thinking of our happiness and joy. He is thinking growth, not diminishment; freedom, not oppression.

That's clear as day if we go back two chapters in St. Luke's Gospel to the other time—the ONLY other time—that Jesus uses those words he addressed to the rich young man: "Sell all you have and give it to the poor." It's in chapter 12 and Jesus is giving a sermon. Listen to what he gives as the reason for his desire that we renounce our possessions. He says, "Fear not, little flock, for it is the Father's good pleasure to give you the Kingdom of Heaven." And it's here that he says, "Sell all you have and give it to the poor." And then he goes on, "Provide yourselves with purses that do not grow old, with a treasure in the heavens that does not fail, where no thief approaches and no moth destroys. For where your treasure is, there will your heart be also."

And earlier in that sermon, Jesus says, "Do not be anxious about your life, what you shall eat, nor about your body, what you shall put on." And then he recalls how God our Father cares for the lilies of the field and the birds of the air, and he asks us to believe that God, our loving Father, will care for us, bringing us finally into his very own Kingdom.

By commending renunciation, then, Jesus is saying, *I don't want you to be anxious about what you have. Don't be captive to your possessions. Don't be their slave—because if that happens to you, then, possessions have become your GOD. They are no longer yours, but you have become theirs. I want you, rather, to be FREE*, Jesus is saying. *Free to follow me, free to love people over things, free to seek the Kingdom of God and its justice—so that all else may be added to you.* It's what Jesus said in the very first Beatitude, "Blessed are the poor in spirit for theirs is the Kingdom of Heaven."

This is not an either-or thing for us. There is no danger that we are choosing or will choose possessions over God one-hundred percent. Hardly. Rather, the question we face is: To what extent have we chosen God over possessions? Do possessions have fifty percent of our heart or twenty percent or five percent, or what? I'm not fully enslaved, but is my right leg in a cast? And, if so, what is the PARTICULAR possession which has me trussed up? Is there something which is a non-negotiable in my life—something I can't imagine forsaking even for God, let alone for the poorest of my neighbors? If so, I'm still crippled, unfree, held captive.

Think about it. And don't be gloomy about it. Look for it with the thought that, having found it, you will be a freer, more peaceful, and more loving person.

And so, let's pray for one another . . . that we may have a first-hand and direct experience of that joy Christ promises to the truly poor of heart. "Blessed are the poor of spirit, for theirs is the Kingdom of God."

24.

When Peter and Jesus Had Words

"You Satan!"

Today's Gospel reading (Mark 8:27-35) is a literary jewel, as well as a profound Christian statement. It is divided into two parts: the first, a dramatic episode, highly charged with feeling; and the second, a theological reflection on the incident by Jesus.

First the drama. It is the interchange between Peter and Jesus, and it unfolds in three short scenes. Each scene revolves around the use of the very same Greek word: *epitimao.* It occurs as the key word in each of the three scenes.

Epitimao is a verb whose first meaning is "to evaluate," "to weigh," or "to estimate." Its second meaning is by far its most common usage, and it is in this second sense that it is used in today's Gospel text. It means: "to evaluate negatively," "to judge critically," "to reprimand, rebuke, reprove, or censure."

In this Gospel reading, we find, first, Jesus "epitimao-ing" or reproving Peter and the apostles. Then, in scene two, we find Peter "epitimao-ing" or reproving Jesus. And, in the third scene, we find Jesus "epitimao-ing" or rebuking just Peter. It is a strong word, denoting confrontation, diametric opposition, conflict, and struggle. It is well chosen for this drama, for the drama is about the very identity, purpose, and mission of Jesus.

Let us see how the drama unfolds.

Jesus asks the apostles, "Who do YOU say that I am?" and Peter, always the impetuous spokesman of the group, responds, "You are the Messiah!" We might have thought that Jesus would be delighted, but it is not that simple. He does indeed accept the title and identification, but he simultaneously rebukes Peter and the others to silence. And his subsequent remarks explain why. He is NOT the Messiah that Peter and the whole Jewish tradition expect. He is not a Messiah come in power to vanquish and scatter Israel's enemies by victorious force. Just the contrary, as he goes on to explain.

He is the Messiah, he says, who will be captured in Jerusalem, who will be brutalized and killed by the High Priests and Elders, and who, through this ignominious experience, will be raised up in glory by his heavenly Father. And it is this dimension of his Messiahship which, as the Gospel notes, Jesus declares openly to his apostles and a great multitude, urging them by example to do the same in others' hearing. He wants to place firm and primary emphasis on the suffering and death he will endure in loving self-sacrifice, for, only in that light, can people call him "Messiah" with the accuracy of truth.

At this message, Peter is aghast. This is not his expectation at all. This is not the kind of Messiah he thought he was joining company with. Nor does it augur the kind of discipleship that he had imagined for himself. "It cannot be," Peter feels. Jesus HAS to be mistaken. Perhaps, it is just a passing mood of depression, discouragement, or despondency.

So, Peter rebukes Jesus. That's the second *epitimao*. We can hear him say, partially in encouragement, partially in shock and dismay, "No, this cannot be. This WILL not be. You SHALL NOT die." In light of Jesus' subsequent response, Peter's statements must have sounded to him like those of the serpent in the Garden of Eden. Satan said to Adam and Eve, "No, you shall not die if you disobey God." Or, like the temptations Satan offered Jesus in the desert after his baptism and before his public ministry. Satan had urged Jesus to become the Messiah of popular expectations: glamorous, dazzling in power, exercising dominion over all nations.

It is exactly in this Satanic way that Jesus obviously understands Peter's remonstrance. Jesus hears and sees Peter as the unwitting puppet of Satan and the spirit of this world—the spirit which puts self-preservation at the top of human values. So, Jesus turns on Peter with a savagery he reserves only for Satan. He gives Peter his most powerful rebuke recorded in Scripture. "You Satan," he calls Peter. "You are not judging by God's standards, but by those of this world."

I believe that part of Jesus' fury comes from the fact that by his advice Peter would have killed Jesus more devastatingly than the High Priest was soon to do. Notice the irony and evil of Peter's remark. He is urging Jesus to preserve his life, but, by so doing, Jesus would surely have LOST his life—the only life that is worth having, his life in God, his life of obedience, his life of fidelity to his very being as Son of God on a mission of salvation to the world. Poor Peter. So misguided. But, also, so teachable. And that is why Jesus reacts so vehemently to Peter.

But then Jesus goes on gently in the second part of our Gospel reading, to give Peter and the others instruction. He reflects on the root of their differences. And in the wake of such a violent confrontation over the life-and-death issue on which the spirit of the world and the Christian life are joined in mortal conflict, Jesus' brief reflection must have made a lasting impression.

Jesus puts it quite simply: "Anyone who seeks to save his own life"—are you listening, Peter?—"will lose it. Whereas the one who loses his life—in surrender to God's will—saves it." Self-preservation is self-destruction. Seek self, and you lose self. Seek God, and you save self. God's glorification is our glorification.

And that—paradoxical as it sounds—is the lasting message which is bequeathed to us today. Amen!

25.

"All Sorts" Day

Celebrating the Saints and Recalling their Sins

Father [Thomas] Gavigan gave me a joke to get me started on this homily. "The Christians in heaven are All Saints. The Christians in Purgatory are All Souls. And the Christians on earth are All Sorts."

Well, believe it or not, I think there is a point to it, too. Before the Saints GOT to heaven, they were certainly of ALL SORTS when they were here on earth. In fact, they were such a mixture of odd sorts that, on the face of it, you might be tempted to wonder how they got to be saints at all.

I can think of a few right off the top of my head, and each of you can probably think of others.

How about the great Saint Peter? Midway in his public life Jesus declared Peter the Rock on whom the entire Church would be built, and this because of the firmness of Peter's faith. On the eve of Jesus' death, not a year later, Peter denies he ever knew the man. An odd sort to be declared a saint.

And remember Saint Paul—and that terrible argument he had with Barnabas about the latter's cousin Mark who had deserted them in the course of a mission journey? "After a violent quarrel," we're told, "they parted company." When you read the Epistles, it seems like Paul is always having a quarrel with someone. And he gets so defensive. Again, an odd sort to be declared a saint.

And then there was Jerome whom we celebrated recently. He had a great mind, no doubt, especially in Scripture studies; but he had an enormous temper, as well, and the way he excoriated those who disagreed with him may well have cost him the papacy, some people feel.

We celebrated Saint Augustine early in September, and we'll remember that after he was ordained a priest, the first two people he received into the Church were his former mistress and his illegitimate son. Now how in the world can the Church declare the likes of him a saint?

We could go on and on. The list is endless of people who have been canonized saints and yet whose faults and weaknesses and sins are glaring. The reason we could go on and on is that this is true of EVERY SAINT IN THE CALENDAR, every saint in heaven. EVERY SAINT was a sinner. In fact, what MADE them a saint was the fact that they RECOGNIZED and ACKNOWLEDGED their sinfulness (that's step one) and turned to God for His forgiveness and glorifying love (that's step two). They OPENED themselves to the power of God's saving and raising love, by confessing themselves needy and sinful children of His. And, in their sinfulness, he loved them; in their weakness, he lifted them; in their desire, he fulfilled them. And therefore, they are saints.

So, when we celebrate the saints, all the saints, we celebrate God and His love for all of us.

When I was in the novitiate 40 years ago, our novice master told us a story. There was a certain nun whom lots of people began to revere as a saint. Her reputation spread far and wide and it was really turning into quite a hubbub. So, the bishop thought he really had to look into this, and one day he paid a visit to the convent and asked to see the sister about whom everyone was talking. When the sister arrived in the front parlor where the bishop was waiting, he asked, "Are you the saint?" The sister answered, "Yes, I am." "That's all I wanted to know," the bishop said. And off he went. He had his answer.

Our novice master went on to tell us the moral of this story: If we are really on the road to sanctity, we won't have the slightest inkling that we are becoming saints at all.

I've always found some consolation in that. How about you?

PART III

Mission ...

Contemplation and Action, in a Troubled World

26.
What Kind of Person is the Jesuit?

Letter from the New Maryland Provincial, 1969

Dear Brothers in Christ,

. . . . What characterizes the Jesuit in a distinguishing manner from the Dominican, the Franciscan, etc.? What identifies the Jesuit *as Jesuit*? Possibly at the risk of oversimplification, I would submit that the distinguishing note of a Jesuit is that he is called by God's grace to that quality of mystical contemplation which was granted to St. Ignatius. He is our Founder not only in the sense that he was the original and dominant figure in the organization of a social body of men, but much more significantly in the sense that every Jesuit is from his entrance formed in the pattern of the mystical experience of St. Ignatius, particularly as it is synthesized in the Spiritual Exercises. We are formed in his spirit; our lives are rooted in his spirituality, and it is his spirituality that qualifies quite distinctively our very personalities.

Each religious order in the Church is distinguished from others, basically by the charismata and graces which distinguish their Founders. Dominic was not Ignatius, nor was Ignatius Francis. Each of them in his own life and spirituality was a prism through which was peculiarly refracted, for their companions and followers, the inexhaustible life of Christ, the Light of the World. While all are thoroughly Christian, spirituality differs from spirituality as Founder differs from Founder, and what characterizes the Jesuit fundamentally is a spirituality that is accurately and fully Ignatian. This spirituality qualifies the Jesuit's very personality, informs and shapes his existence, so that he is—and should be—notably a different *kind of person*, a different kind of Christian, than his non-Jesuit peers.

What kind of person is the Jesuit? Properly understood, with all that it implies, the traditional description says it in a nutshell: the Jesuit is *"contemplativus in actione"* [a contemplative in action]. The Jesuit *contemplativus*. He is a man who seeks and experiences the divine Presence and Power often, regularly, and pervasively in contemplation, in prayer, alone and in isolation. He is a man of rich inwardness, who does not flee from the Emptiness, the Silence, and the restless Urging deep within himself, but embraces It, allows himself to be taken up by It, surrenders himself to It, as to the Presence of God's creative Word at the core of his being. As a contemplative, the Jesuit is not afraid to stand nakedly in prayer before the Silence which is spoken at the very deepest level of his being, for he knows that this Silence is the Word of God which is summoning him, revealing Itself to him, and revealing him to himself. He listens quietly and allows this Silence to speak, surrenders to Its promise and submits to Its judgment. He lets go of himself, knowing full well that this self-surrender will lead him to death—to the death of selfishness, of personal preference, of vanities, and "security blankets"—to a death which will be Christ's glorification in him, and thus his own death-glorification.

As a contemplative, the Jesuit is the man who, ever more so, grows more fully conscious and aware of the Presence of this Mysterious Word in his existence. Christ literally grows in him, emerges in his consciousness. Like the leaven in the loaf, the Christ-life of the Word begins to permeate his consciousness, not as a direct object of attention or a thing [of] thought, but as the living hue or horizon, the qualifying coloring of every thought or deed. His world becomes consciously Christic.

As a religious contemplative, the Jesuit is a man for whom celibacy is a *conditio sine qua non* for the quality of prayer he prays. Though he is affable, outgoing, and lovingly concerned for others, though he enjoys support and consolation in community and common prayer, his life is necessarily and essentially one of **radical solitude,** a solitude he does not expect—does not want—Jesuit community or any other relationships, however close, to eradicate. As a man given over to death in life ("Into thy hands I commend my spirit"), he faces his God alone in life, as indeed he will at death. The non-celibate Jesuit is a contradiction in terms, just as the non-contemplative Jesuit celibate is an impossibility. When the contemplation goes, celibacy will not be far behind, because the Jesuit—the

Ignatian—grace, which alone can sustain him, has gone out of a man's life.

Thus, the Jesuit is essentially a man of prayer, of contemplation, of growing and continual awareness of and surrender to the Word of Silence which prompts, impels, sustains, consoles, and enlightens him at the lowest and most fundamental reach of his human existence. To attain such prayerfulness, some quiet is requisite, as well as reflection, planning, patience, and time. There is required a process of *removens prohibens,* of discarding the impediments, to the emergence of Christ's Presence to ourselves. Some discipline and asceticism must structure our lives, regulate our thoughts and desires, liberate us from ourselves. With the help of God's grace and inspiration, we must consciously and systematically dispose ourselves in order to experience the ever fuller manifestation and revelation of God's presence in us. Here we have the masterful techniques which St. Ignatius has bequeathed us in the Exercises.

What this ascetical process of self-disposition for contemplative experience of God will mean practically for each of us in terms of time-order, work-load, sleep, food, drink, entertainment, companionship, reading, etc., is either too obvious (on the basis of *tantum-quantum* and detachment) or too personal to warrant discussion here. This *removens prohibens* is the function of the Examination of Conscience, which we make systematically twice a day.

Just as, for the Jesuit, a process of asceticism is personal and varied according to temperament and need, so too is his method of attaining contemplative union with God personal and varied. We know that although Ignatius insisted that his followers be men intimately one with God, he not only tolerated but also encouraged a great variety of methods and techniques for achieving this union. Ignatius had a genius for adaptability, experimentation, open readiness to the movement of the Spirit in particular persons, times, places, and circumstances, as is clear in the Exercises. The prayer that is "good for me now" is the prayer which is now bearing fruit in my life. To discover this is again a function of the Examen, but also, and perhaps particularly, of spiritual direction and the account of conscience.

Mystical contemplation—in the pattern of St. Ignatius and to the degree that God grants—is an attainable gift for each Jesuit. It is not only **not** a "far-out" fringe possibility, but also the indispensable presupposition of the Jesuit life. Ignatius presumes it in the formed Jesuit. It is the aim of the Exercises to bring a man to this contemplative, immediate, experiential presence and to God's Word. He speaks of "feeling It intimately" (*intime sentire*), "tasting" (*gustans*), "touching" (*tangere*), etc., when struggling to describe the direct manifestation of God in a man's consciousness. Moreover, the whole process of discernment and election, which should govern the life of each Jesuit and the Society at large, presumes immediate contemplative experience of God as is evident in Ignatius' description of election (Exercises, #175-188; cf. K. Rahner, "Individual Knowledge in Ignatius Loyola," *The Dynamic Element in the Church,* Herder and Herder, 1964, pp. 84-170). Ignatian election is not a rational process through to logical conclusion, but a decision of appropriateness before the Light of God's intimate Presence. Thus, to live, to choose, to discern, and to act *as a Jesuit* presumes a degree—a rather high, and growing, degree—of mystical contemplation.

This is the first step in the characterization of a Jesuit, namely, that he is *contemplativus,* but it does not yet distinguish and identify the Jesuit. Others are contemplative also, but what is unique about the Jesuit, what is remarkably innovative in Ignatius' time, is that the Jesuit is *contemplativus IN ACTIONE.*

Crucial here is the realization that for Ignatius contemplation and action are not two distinct and disparate realities. Rather, contemplation and action are two aspects, two phases, two (philosophical) "moments" of the *one* Jesuit life. To contemplate is to be *in action.* It is an *act.* Though wrought in solitude and inwardness, the self-surrendering "Yes" before Mystery (which prayer is) is a most vital, a most self-integrating, self-dispositive, and indeed a most agonizing *act.* Prayer essentially is not thinking *about* God, self, and neighbor. It is an active self-surrender to the *God* Who is equally bodied forth in my *neighbor.* Thus, prayer is living action, wrenchingly so, as fully conscious and as freely self-dispository as is possible at this moment of my existence. . . .

Jesuit contemplation inherently tends to service, realizes itself in service, and "becomes itself" in service. So true is this that a Jesuit who is not in *in actione,* i.e., thoroughly, joyfully, and compassionately in service to others, is clearly not a Jesuit *contemplativus.* Between the "moments" of contemplative prayer and loving service, there is for the Jesuit a reciprocally enriching and fulfilling dialectic.

Just as contemplation is action, so active service is contemplative, because Christ's presence, power, and being consciously pervades all. The Jesuit who is *contemplativus in actione* is no less conscious of the Christic presence in the neighbor he serves, than he is in the reaches of contemplative prayer. The obverse is also true: one who is not continually conscious of Christ's presence in contemplation will not recognize and hence will not render loving and compassionate service to Christ in his neighbor. Each "moment" enriches, sustains, and complements the other, for man's being is originally *one*: spirit (indissolubly unique and autonomous) incarnate (ineradicably social).

The beauty of Ignatian spirituality is that it avoids both of two possible and unfortunate extremes: (1) Though it lays heavy stress on the contemplative, it avoids individualistic piety of the "Jesus and me" brand—a piety which is fundamentally un-Christian and self-seeking—since it is radically other-directed and service-oriented; (2) Though it is a spirituality for mobile, active, and thoroughly apostolic men, it avoids the pitfall of activism, social Gospel-ism or any taint of *effusion ad exteriora.* Based as it is on a thoroughly Christian understanding of the Incarnation (and hence of the nature of man), it recognizes the essential and original unity of contemplation and action, blending both aspects for a life more apostolically active than the activist's, and more thoroughly self-integrating than the individualist's. It frees man totally for the secular, because it anchors him absolutely in Christ. Were Ignatius' life and spirituality not the fruit of divine inspiration we could call it a work of genius. Perhaps we can call it both.

This, then, is the Jesuit: *contemplativus in actione.* He is a *kind of person* with a quality of personality bred of divine grace, the very grace of Ignatius, Ignatian grace. There is nothing external that necessarily and inevitably characterizes him. Quite the contrary, he is a man of such indifference, such mobility, such detachment, humility and flexibility that he or his brothers can be expected to be doing anything, wearing anything, living anywhere, so long as there is hope of God's greater glory and fuller service to men. What makes him a Jesuit is the person he has become—or more accurately, that God has made him—in the pattern of Ignatius. As Father General remarked to the American Provincials in Rome recently, of the Jesuit it can be said, *"Ama, et fac quod vis."* He is a man so one with Christ in contemplative action that whatever he does is a Jesuit deed. If this is the Jesuit, then it is for men suited for this life that we pray on this feast of the Sacred Heart. This is the call, the vocation, that God is making, to generous young men through us as secondary causes and instruments of His Will.

We will attract Jesuits as powerfully as we are Jesuits. It is the message of the Incarnation that our tepidity, our timidity, our mediocrity, and our worldliness *can* and *do* "shorten God's arm." On the other hand, if the Christ Who is our Life, radiates with warmth, with kindness, with self-deprecating zeal in our very being and activity, we can be sure that God, in His generosity, will bless our numbers.

Excerpted from Father Jim Connor's first letter as provincial to members of the Maryland Province of the Society of Jesus, June 13, 1969.

27.

Becoming a "Person for Others"

An Ignatian Discernment

In an oft-quoted speech to alumni of Jesuit schools, in Valencia, Spain, on July 31, 1973, Father General Pedro Arrupe said that the goal of our Jesuit educational apostolate is to produce "Men for Others." It quickly became translated as "Persons for Others."

By "Persons for Others," he didn't mean people who occasionally or even often did charitable acts for others, but people whose whole life-orientation was concern for others. And in that sense, they ARE "persons for others." They are NOT persons whose life perspective is SELF-promotion, much less SELF-gratification. Father Arrupe's description of Jesuit mission soon became the focus, not just of Jesuit education, but of ALL of our Jesuit ministries: parishes, retreat houses, social centers, and other works.

The ideal of becoming a "Person for Others" didn't originate with Father Pedro Arrupe, however. It originated with St. Ignatius Loyola—in his own conversion experience from self-promotion to service. Ignatius' conversion experience is the central grace of the Society of Jesus, of all its ministries, and of all of us, Jesuit and lay, who live out, promote, and offer to others our Ignatian service.

So to strengthen our own sense of identity and mission, let's recall once again Ignatius' conversion, which is described in his quasi-autobiography, *St. Ignatius's Own Story*, as told to Luis Gonzalez de Camara. The opening sentences read:

> Up to his twenty-sixth year he was a man given over to the vanities of the world, who took a special delight in the exercise of arms, with a great and vain desire of winning glory.

Indeed, up to his mid-twenties, Ignatius was driven by ambition and vanity. He was a showoff. Born in 1491, the youngest son of a Basque nobleman, serving first as a courtier and then a soldier, Ignatius was convinced that his life—if not the whole world—revolved around himself. He was hardly "a man for others!"

This life orientation and the self-image that went with it were crushed when both of his legs were shattered by a cannonball at a battle against French invaders in the city of Pamplona in northern Spain. His legs were so crippled that Ignatius' chivalrous showoff days were over. To what should he turn now? This was the question he pondered as he lay recovering from several painful surgeries in the family castle at Loyola. His wondering was mostly in the form of daydreams about "what ifs."

Let's go to his autobiography and hear his own description of this experience:

> He had been much given to reading worldly books of fiction and knight errantry, and feeling well enough to read he asked for some of these books to help while away the time. In that house, however, they could find none of those he was accustomed to read, and so they gave him a Life of Christ and a book of the Lives of the Saints in Spanish.
>
> By the frequent reading of these books he conceived some affection for what he found there narrated. Pausing in his reading, he gave himself up to thinking over what he had read.
>
> At other times he dwelt on the things of the world which formerly had occupied his thoughts. Of the many vain things that presented themselves to him, one took such possession of his heart that without realizing it he could spend two, three, or even four hours on end thinking of it, fancying what he would have to do in the service of a certain lady, of the means he would take to reach the country where she was living, of the verses, the promises he would make her, the deeds of gallantry he would do in her service. He was so enamored with all this that he did not see how impossible it would all be, because the lady was of no

ordinary rank; neither countess, nor duchess, but of a nobility much higher than any of these.

Nevertheless, our Lord came to his assistance, for He saw to it that these thoughts were succeeded by others that sprang from the things he was reading. In reading the Life of our Lord and the Lives of the Saints, he paused to think and reason with himself. "Suppose that I should do what St. Francis did, what St. Dominic did?" He thus let his thoughts run over many things that seemed good to him, always putting before himself things that were difficult and important which seemed to him easy to accomplish when he proposed them. But all his thought was to tell himself, "St. Dominic did this; therefore, I must do it. St. Francis did this; therefore, I must do it."

These thoughts also lasted a good while. And then other things taking their place, the worldly thoughts above mentioned came upon him and remained a long time with him. This succession of diverse thoughts was of long duration, and they were either of worldly achievements which he desired to accomplish, or those of God which took hold of his imagination to such an extent that, worn out with the struggle, he turned them all aside and gave his attention to other things.

But eventually he noticed this difference in his daydreaming:

a. "When he was thinking of the things of the world he was filled with delight, but when afterwards he dismissed them from weariness, he was dry and dissatisfied."

b. "But when he thought of going barefoot to Jerusalem and of eating nothing but herbs and performing the other rigors he saw that the saints had performed, he was consoled; not only when he entertained these thoughts, but even after dismissing them he remained cheerful and satisfied."

He paid no attention to this, however, "nor did he stop to weigh the difference until one day his eyes were opened a little and he began to wonder at the difference and to reflect on it, learning from experience that:

a. "one kind of thoughts left him sad and

b. "the other cheerful."

The book continues: "Thus, step-by-step, he came to recognize the difference between the two spirits that moved him, the one being from the evil spirit, the other from God." And there's more:

> He acquired no little light from this insight and began to think more seriously of his past life and the great need he had of doing penance for it. It was during his reading that these desires of imitating the saints came to him. . . . What he desired most of all to do, as soon as he was restored to health, was to go to Jerusalem . . . undertaking all the disciplines and abstinences which a generous soul on fire with the love of God is wont to desire.
>
> The thoughts (. . . and images and attractions) of the past were soon forgotten in the presence of these holy desires, and they were confirmed by a spiritual experience, in this manner. One night while he was awake he saw clearly an image of Our Lady with the holy child Jesus. From this sight he received for a considerable time very great consolation, and he was left with a loathing for his whole past life. . . .

There are several key things happening to Ignatius here which will make a lasting impression on him and which will shape his future life in service to others. To mention a few:

1. We see the personal conversion taking place before our eyes as he records this experience. His conversion will be from the "vanities of the world" and his "great and vain desire of winning glory" to concern for others in the example of Jesus, Dominic, and Francis. His desire was to become "A Man for Others," as Father Arrupe would put it centuries later. And for Ignatius it was a 180-degree reorientation—even though, as he will shortly realize, it is still tinged with some vanity.

2. Notice how indispensably important his feelings are in en-

abling him to choose this change of life. His initial excitement about doing great deeds for his noble lady eventually sours in his stomach. Vainglory doesn't sustain him. The peace, joy, and satisfaction at sacrificing for the good of others in the model of Jesus and the saints persist and continue to sustain him well after his reading about them.

3. On reflection, he begins to discover the sources of these two different sets of feelings. The source of the feelings of peace and quiet joy at the prospect of service is the "good spirit," while the source of his original delight at impressing the lady, which eventually becomes emptiness and dissatisfaction, is the "evil spirit." These spirits are of God and Satan.

4. Ignatius eventually was able to describe quite clearly and accurately these "movements of spirit." His experience of Satan's invitations he called "desolation" and his experience of God's invitations he called "consolation." And he came to call this process of recognition "discernment of spirits."

5. This process of discernment of spirits will become central to Ignatian spirituality and to the whole Jesuit tradition. It is the process of recognizing and embracing the invitations that God is offering to us to JOIN Jesus on his mission of helping our human family to become the Kingdom of God, a Kingdom of peace and justice, compassion and love and mutual support—especially for those most in need. In other words, through discernment of spirits, Ignatius was guided with accuracy to join Jesus on mission. And so it will be for all his followers.

6. People living Ignatian spirituality are not simply "contemplatives," like Trappists. They are "contemplatives IN ACTION," that is, in apostolic service to others. Ignatian spirituality is mission-oriented spirituality. We discern spirits in order to discover where and how God is leading us to serve others.

And we respond with God's grace—as "Persons for Others."

Excerpted from a talk at St. Ignatius Church in Baltimore on July 27, 2012.

28.
Companions on Mission
A New Era of Lay-Jesuit Collaboration

In recent times, one of the most exciting developments in the Society of Jesus has been the growing emphasis on lay-Jesuit companionship in mission. The various forms of partnership between Jesuits and our lay collaborators promise even greater growth and new patterns of relationship well into the future.

I keep thinking, "We've come a long way since the good old days when I was a boy." I can still hear my father, who used to love to say that the role of laypeople in the church could be summarized in three words: "pray, pay, and obey." There are some people in the Church—and some of them may be in leadership roles!—who think that is still true. But, if we look, not just at lay-Jesuit relationships, but at the Church in the trenches, at the grass roots, in the parishes, in the schools, in the retreat houses, in the social centers, we will find that that is no longer the case at all.

The point is made clearly in a book by Paul Wilkes entitled *Excellent Catholic Parishes,* subtitled *The Guide to Best Places and Practices.* It is about parishes and parish life in the United States, and he visited and surveys a whole host of them from coast to coast. He lists the eighteen traits that excellent parishes have in common, and names the parishes across the country that exemplify those traits in their vibrant liturgical life and service to others. Listen to what he has to say about the ideal relationship between clergy and laity.

> Excellent parishes do not *allow* laypeople to do what was once the province of ordained clergy and vowed religious. . . . Priests honestly see laywomen and men as equals, and laypeople not

only seek to exercise their rights but accept responsibilities. The issue becomes one of acknowledging individual talents, seeing who can best do the job. There is no bemoaning the shrinking number of priests in excellent parishes; the work is naturally apportioned among lay and ordained. Once these "people of God" (as Vatican II pronounces all believers and seekers) are freed to express themselves, a veritable explosion of talent occurs. Every parish in this book gives testimony to that (p. 165).

The same could be said of education. Years ago, when I first started teaching as a twenty-four-year-old Jesuit scholastic at Gonzaga College High School in Washington, D.C., we had a handful of excellent lay teachers and the best lay registrar I have ever known. But it was clear whose school it really was and who called the shots. There were no lay members of the board of directors; in fact, I am not even sure we had a board of directors, much less did we have an academic council that would represent faculty viewpoint to the administration when policy decisions were being made. And, of course, all administrators were Jesuit.

By contrast—and probably the starkest contrast to date—is the situation now at Georgetown University where a layperson, John "Jack" DeGioia, is president. He is a wonderful person, deeply steeped in Jesuit spirituality, having made the full 30-day retreat of the Spiritual Exercises years before he ever dreamed he would be president of Georgetown. As a student, as a professor, and as a dean, he imbibed the Ignatian educational pedagogy. Who could be better suited to the responsibilities of president?

But as soon as his appointment was announced, some people raised the question, "Isn't it a failure on the part of Jesuits not to have seen to it that a Jesuit was named president of Georgetown?" There are good, thoughtful people on both sides of that debate. Personally, I am not in that debate. I reason this way. The search committee and the board of directors and Jesuit superiors—all those involved in the decision, in other words—are all people of enormous integrity with deep devotion to the Jesuit ideals of Georgetown University. They decided, out of their Ignatian way of discerning, what they honestly felt was best for the University, given the timing, the pool of applicants, and other specifics of the situation. On those grounds, I regard the decision as the work of the Spirit. It is but another instance of how the Spirit is nudging us to join together as lay and Jesuit in our shared commitment to service and mission in the Ignatian tradition.

Historically speaking, how did we come to this new realization and sense of lay-Jesuit relationship? Are there any social, personal, cultural factors—through which the Spirit works—which help us to understand and explain it?

Let me just tick off a few things that occur to me. You probably can think of more or better explanations.

- Better educated Catholic laypeople since the early 1900s, maybe even since the 1950s, owing in part to the GI Bill of Rights, which helped usher in upward social mobility and responsibility.
- More *consciously* spiritual laypeople—for instance, the experience of making retreats and the Spiritual Exercises.
- Religious and theological education (contrast my grandfather who would have bloodied any nose in the bar that denied papal infallibility, even though he hadn't the foggiest idea what it meant. He just knew that "we" held that belief).
- The availability of books and magazines on religion and society (*America* magazine, *Commonweal,* diocesan newspapers, the *National Catholic Reporter,* etc.).
- Former priests and religious in the pews and the classrooms and social centers. A rich asset for the renewal of the Church.
- Vatican Council II—the groundbreaking way it conceived the Church, as, for instance, the People of God, the era of the laity. Consider a horizontal structure of the Church, with responsibility spread among the laity, as distinct from a vertical structure. I like to call it the "pancake" image of the Church versus the "triangle" image—though my friend Nita Crowley at Holy Trinity parish, where I was pastor, wryly observed that there is never one pancake on a plate, and "I know who the top pancake is!"
- The appreciation, theologically and sociologically, of the lay

state, of marriage as a sacrament and the sanctity of family, the priesthood of all the baptized, the vocation of Christian service in the world—in the world of politics, business, media, banking, international development, and so on.

- The social consciousness—and conscience—that is awakened in us by modern media and other forms of communication that literally bring wars, famines, AIDs epidemics, and human poverty and squalor right into our living rooms. There is the travel we do, the emails we receive, the Internet sites we search. We are so much better informed that, as sensitive Catholics, we cannot but ask, "What must I DO?" And we find ways of volunteering our services or even of changing our primary occupation—sometimes as companions, lay and Jesuit, with one another.

- The realization on the part of priests and religious that most of the challenges and opportunities that the Church now faces simply cannot be met—or even understood—without the perspective, the expertise, the life experience, and the specialized knowledge and skills that laypeople can bring to them. Example: my principal work at the Woodstock Theological Center at Georgetown University for the past fifteen years was coordinating ethics projects with lay professionals in business, health care, lobbying, government and civil society, the global economy, and so on. Bringing Gospel values to these areas absolutely demands the expertise, the experience, and the savvy of lay professionals—who bring a competence that few priests and religious have. Therefore, we need lay partnership in mission.

- De-clericalization by priests and religious—certainly by Jesuits. I think of "de-clericalization" as "getting off the pedestal" and rejoining the human race. It is with "real" people versus staying in the cloister or on the campus or in the rectory—and having them always come to us ("See me in the parlor!"). An example would be the contrast between Jesuit life at Loyola College of Maryland when I taught there in the 1960s and today, in areas like dress, mobility, associations, and the very grounds of our relationships.

- Even the recent scandals in the Church can be an occasion for deepened humility, open honesty, admission of ignorance and sinfulness, acceptance of a shared and common humanity, an expression of remorse and apology, and a request for help. And with it might come a much more accurate theological understanding of being human together, of needing one another, of the permanence of change, development, and evolution. All of that opens the door to more relaxed and fruitful companionship between priests and religious AND laypeople. Let's face it: the most glorious characteristic of my existence is not ordination to the priesthood. It is not being vowed to religious life. It is the unbelievable gift that we all share in common: our humanity. That is to say, it is that we, all of us together, are made in the image and likeness of God and, through Christ, have become and are brothers and sisters to one another, with God as our Father.

Finally, how is the effort to enter into genuine lay-Jesuit partnership going to change us? What does it demand of us? Why is it scary, yet so promising, at the same time? How will our new relationships with one another influence and deepen our relationship with God?

These are the questions that came up and were considered in Decree 13 of the 1995 Jesuit General Congregation 34. What they said about lay-Jesuit collaboration was groundbreaking, unprecedented. The opening paragraph of this Decree on "Cooperation with the Laity in Mission" states the *fact* and the Jesuit *commitment*. The fact is that this is and will progressively become ever more so "The Church of the Laity." The commitment is the Jesuit resolve to cooperate and support laypersons in their new roles of leadership in the Church.

The challenge to Jesuits and the need for them to undergo a conversion and transformation of attitude is laid out quite frankly in another part of Decree 13. On the flip side, it suggests what Jesuits hope laity will feel called to undertake.

The emerging "Church of the Laity" will also have an impact on our own Jesuit apostolic works. This transformation can enrich these works and expand their Ignatian character, if we know how to cooperate with the grace of the emergence of the laity. When we speak of "our apostolates," we will mean something different by "our." It will signify a genuine Ignatian partnership of laity and Jesuits, each of us acting according to our proper vocation. Laypersons will rightly take on a greater role of responsibility and leadership within these works. Jesuits will be called on to support them in their initiative by Ignatian formation, inculcation of Jesuit apostolic values, and the witness of our priestly and religious lives. If our service will be humbler, it will also be more challenging and creative, and more in accord with the graces we have received. This actualization of the vocation of the laity can show more clearly the grace of our vocation (#20).

In an earlier section of the same decree, there is a description of how we Jesuits can assist laypersons in their roles of leadership in the mission of the Church.

The Society of Jesus places itself at the service of this mission of the laity by offering what we are and have received: our spiritual and apostolic inheritance, our educational resources, and our friendship. We offer Ignatian spirituality as a specific gift to animate the ministry of the laity. This apostolic spirituality respects the unique spirituality of the individual and adapts itself to present needs; it helps persons to discern their call and "in all things to love and serve the Divine Majesty." We offer to laity the practical wisdom we have learned from more than four centuries of apostolic experience. Through our schools, universities, and other educational programs we make pastoral and theological training available. Perhaps most importantly, we join with them in companionship: serving together, learning from and responding to each other's concerns and initiatives, dialoguing with one another on apostolic objectives (#7).

Finally, another section of this Decree is again, quite frank with Jesuits about how this collaboration with laity is going to stretch them, sometimes perhaps painfully so.

> Cooperation with laity in mission requires the formation and renewal of all Jesuits. . . . Ongoing formation in apostolic situations—if we listen to others, learn from their spirituality, and face together the difficulties of genuine cooperation—will deepen this capacity. Both in our initial and ongoing formation, laypeople can help us understand and respect their distinct vocation as well as appreciate our own (#9).

What is the ultimate grounding of our collaboration with one another—our bonding in a unity of service? It is the "way of proceeding," the spirituality and the style of leadership and service, which is so typically Ignatian and yet adaptable to both the Jesuit life and lay life. Father General Peter-Hans Kolvenbach identified this core of our companionship in a talk he gave to the Lay Partners of Jesuits in Venezuela a few years ago. He first catalogues a series of successful initiatives in which Jesuits and many laypeople had collaborated as partners: educational enterprises, social services, spirituality centers, and so on. Then he took this collaboration a step forward—to its core. This is what he said:

> All of this sharing through the years culminated in 1996 in the *Comision Jesuitas-Laicas-Laicos*. This began a process of apostolic deliberation in which all together desire to find what God wants of the Province of Venezuela in the next years. It is nothing less than inviting the laity to search for what God wants of the Company of Jesus in Venezuela in the third millennium. Doing this means choosing a long and difficult journey; that of communitarian discernment, that of the shared search for the will of God. Indeed, this entails an invitation into the heart of the Company of Jesus, into the great secret of the Jesuits—actually, the only secret!

Father Kolvenbach says here that it is our Ignatian discerning and deciding together how God is calling us to mission that roots, grounds, unifies, and forges us as companions. When the discerning and deciding is Ignatian, then the mission is Ignatian, and so too are the "missionaries," both lay and Jesuit in companionship together.

Where do we get facility in this kind of discerning, deciding, and doing? We get it with practice, and the "playbook" is called "the Spiritual Exercises" of St. Ignatius. Doing the Exercises is the training program. In a nutshell, the Exercises relieve us of our fears and intimidations and lift us to the freedom of the Children of God. We come to this peaceful self-acceptance and self-confidence, because the Exercises help us realize, accept, and rejoice in the absolutely unswerving and unconditional love of God for us. However sinful or weak we have been or are, God's love is constant—constantly understanding and forgiving. Ours simply to accept it. What a consoling, yet demanding, grace that is! And with Christ we want to shout this Good News from the rooftops. That is the "mission" we feel impelled to embark upon.

Yet as soon as we do—as soon as Christ did—a certain segment of the population reacts defensively, angrily, even violently. And we come then to appreciate the reason for Christ's persecution, and eventual execution. And then we know that this is the path we are called to follow with him—not with bitterness, much less with anger, but with the conviction that forgiveness, not retaliation or vengeance, is the road to peace, to the building up of the Kingdom of God, to genuine "full development."

And isn't that what life's all about? It is certainly the core of our Christian calling and mission—whatever form it may take.

Excerpted from the Annual Ignatian Lecture at St. Ignatius Church, Baltimore, July 28, 2003

29.

The Mission of a Jesuit Business School

Unique? Why?

What makes the business school at a Jesuit university so attractive, if not unique?

Case in point: the Sellinger School of Business and Management at Loyola University Maryland, where I serve as an adviser and faculty member. It is, to begin with, a liberal arts educational institution. It is not a trade school where people come simply to learn the contemporary tools of business and to master the specific details of the way in which business is done. It does that, of course, but not simply that.

A liberal arts education is concerned not only to tell people how the job is done today but how it was done yesteryear and how it very well might be done 20, 30, or 40 years from now. A liberal arts education aims to get down to the basic foundations of how people work and therefore how, predictably, specific patterns of work will unfold in the future.

The "product" of Loyola's enterprise is not a degree, but a person— the person who is the student today and who will be a leader tomorrow. The saying goes, "Education is what's left when everything you have learned in school has been forgotten." By that, we mean that at some future tomorrow skills will be replaced, content will be out of date, systems will become passé, but the liberally educated person is one who is able to adapt to new times with imagination and innovation, and continue to be a successful leader within his or her company and even beyond their business within society at large.

To study at Loyola's Sellinger School is, therefore, a transformative experience. Our aim is to help people to understand their own gifts, their own promise, their own best way of operating, and the role they play as team members and team leaders. By knowing themselves they can live and work with great self-confidence and with the assurance that they have the resources to respond even to threatening changes of circumstance and whatever else the future may bring.

A Jesuit dictum is that "we train a whole person who is wholly for others." This point is convincingly made by Jim Collins in his book, *Good to Great: Why Some Companies Make the Leap—and Others Don't.* After interviewing and researching many dozens of corporate leaders, he concludes that the really successful CEOs are personally humble and passionately committed to the success of their companies. A greedy person is a loser, he says.

Therefore, one of the main dimensions of a Jesuit education is what is called in the Latin, *cura personalis.* It means care and concern for the person. Since the person is the primary product of this educational enterprise, each member of the staff and faculty is concerned to engage personally with each and every student, ready to listen to where he or she is coming from, so that, in companionship, faculty and staff can assist them and go with them on whichever road they desire to travel in years ahead. Graduation at Loyola never means a parting of the ways. It is a new beginning in personal relationships.

There is also an old saying, "Unless you see your business from the moon, you have it out of focus." A liberal arts education assists people in developing a broad, even comprehensive, perspective not only on their businesses but also upon their own lives. Business aims to flourish within society, within particular cultures, in relationship with many other businesses and under the watchful eye of a certain political system or perhaps many political systems throughout the world. If this is the era of globalization, then every business needs to be able to locate itself where it lives and works on the surface of the globe.

This breadth of perspective is precisely the concern of a liberal arts education—an education that is sometimes called "humanistic" because it is concerned with and about human beings. Our interest—the interest of both student and faculty—is in learning about human beings: who they are, how they work, how they collaborate together and what their deepest desires are for their personal, professional, and social fulfillment.

We are interested not only in a current snapshot of the globe. As a liberal arts educational experience, we are interested in knowing where we have come from historically, where we are right now, and where we very likely are headed in the future. Business has not always been done in the capitalist system. But do we know why capitalism arose? Do we know who the major movers and shakers were? Do we know the glorious assets and the threatening liabilities of the capitalist system? Do we realize how capitalism exists in many different forms across the face of the globe? And do we realize that even American capitalism is undergoing a process of radical change under the pressures and opportunities of the globalization process?

Unless we are aware of the historical and geographical dimensions of economic life and growth, we will not be prepared to be innovative, imaginative, and productive leaders in the years ahead. We need to be people of the past, present, and future—simultaneously—if we are to be the kinds of leaders that successful business requires.

And, finally we need to be "persons for others." "No man is an island," the famous poet John Donne wrote centuries ago. It is equally true that "No business is an island." Donne's point is that each and every human being is essentially social by nature. We were born of a "mommy and daddy"—whether or not they lived under the same roof. Unless someone had fed, warmed, bathed, and otherwise nurtured us we wouldn't have lived for three days. Unless someone had spoken to us, read to us, and continued to educate and socialize us, we would look today like thoroughly intimidated animals in someone's back alley. Without the care of society and our participation in society, we would not be human in any ordinary sense of the word.

And even today we cannot continue to grow and develop as humans unless we are cooperating in the human growth of others and of society at large. Shorthand, the way we GROW UP is by GROWING OUT in our concern and support of OTHERS and in our companionship with them. The Jesuit philosopher, Bernard Lonergan, put it more technically: "Humans achieve authenticity through self-transcendence," i.e., we become ourselves by rising OUT of ourselves and engaging with others.

At Loyola's Sellinger School of Business, concern for others—customers, investors, employees, suppliers, neighbors, and the natural environment—are central, not just for business success, but for the personal and social growth of all involved.

These are not simply things we do, at a Jesuit business school. It is who we believe we are—persons with and for others.

Adapted from an essay produced primarily for Sellinger School faculty and staff.

30.
Theological Reflection
Breaking Open a Definition

Over the past few decades, theological reflection has emerged as an explicit part of the mission of the Society of Jesus. Indeed, the Jesuit organization I direct—the Woodstock Theological Center—was formed specifically in response to the call for "theological reflection on the human problems of today." It was a call originally made by the beloved Jesuit Superior General, Pedro Arrupe. But what exactly is theological reflection? Here's a definition.

> *Theological reflection is working to understand and evaluate an issue or situation from a perspective informed and enlightened by religious faith in order to do what seems best for the improvement of our living together as a human family.*

We can take this definition and break it open for a better understanding by pondering the words used in it.

Working . . .

Theological reflection is an activity that takes work. There are, as we will see, various operations or phases to this work. We say "working" rather than "a work" or "an effort" because it is something that goes on and on, at all times. It is repetitive or cumulative. We humans are always trying to figure something out in order to understand what's going on, so that we can "manage" it better, and do what we think is best.

Understand . . .

Something comes to our attention, like the mass shooting of students at a suburban high school, and we ask, "What is going on here? What is the explanation? Why did it happen? What are we to make of this?" All of these are questions for understanding. The issues will not always be as urgent as school slayings. It might be that we can't find our car keys, so we ask "What is going on here? Where are they?" And we retrace our steps to figure it out.

There are three interrelated phases or movements in understanding: noticing and collecting the data, creating or imagining and proposing the various possible explanations for the data behind the issue or situation, and finally picking—on the basis of the data or evidence—which from among the possible explanations is more accurate. The probability of accuracy can range from tentative to certain, depending on various factors. But there is an urge in us to "get it right," and that's what we are invariably aiming for.

Evaluate . . .

When we have made our judgment about the issue or situation, i.e., when we are satisfied that we have understood what is going on, then the question arises, "What are we to do about it?" Once we have understood that we must have left our keys in the bar, we call the bartender—or we drop by for another drink! Once we explain why the students were killed, we start laying out proposals to prevent such tragedies in the future. The proposal will, of course, depend on what you deem the basic cause to be: you could call for gun control, regulating violence in movies, video games, and television, charging parents with the children's crimes, working to improve the general culture in the U.S., or something else. We want to know what to do about things, and the action chosen is meant to promote certain values or to prevent certain ills.

The phases or movements in "evaluation" are: (1) recalling the understanding or judgment of "What is really going on here," (2) proposing the various ways in which we might remedy the situation, (3) weighing the relative merits of the various proposed courses of action, (4) deciding which is the best or the better.

Issue or situation . . .

The issue or situation could be in any sphere of life: personal, family, work-related, political, economic, social, cultural, or religious. In every sphere of our lives, questions arise spontaneously: "What's going on here" and "Does it need improvement—and, if so, what?" Depending on a person's occupation or profession, loyalties and commitments, some issues or situations will emerge as more pressing than others. Issues that look trivial or non-existent to some people are quite urgent and very important to other people. This variation is often tied to one's perspective, which needs explanation.

From a perspective...

Each of us has a particular perspective from within which we view life, rank/order important things, pass judgments on issues and people, make sense of our world, and even know who we are as individuals. These are some of the various ways our perspective "works" for us. But the perspective itself is hard to grab hold of because it is made up of often-unnoticed and unexamined suppositions, presumptions, beliefs, values, and opinions that we have mostly inherited from our families, peers, teachers, or churches. Perspective is the product of many things: experience, nationality, religious affiliation, education, profession or line of work, siblings, political affiliation, economic class, neighborhood and social milieu, date of birth and historical era, current age, and a host of other things. Within and as part of our perspective are the meanings that are our key to explaining what's going on and the values which motivate the actions we choose to take.

Your perspective grows and expands over the course of a lifetime. As you move from job to job and accumulate more work experience, you see things from a richer and broader perspective and can make wiser and more accurate business judgments. If you travel around and come to experience other cultures, languages, ways of doing things, your perspective gets richer and broader. You are less parochial and more cosmopolitan. As your newspaper reading moves beyond the comics and the sports or style sections to national and international news, your "world" literally gets bigger. And as your concern and compassion for people in that bigger world get deeper and more sensitive—especially for women and children who bear the brunt of poverty, starvation, illiteracy, and squalor—your broader perspective enables you to understand and evaluate situations and issues more realistically and accurately.

Informed and enlightened by religious faith . . .

Our perspective is informed and enlightened by many life experiences. You may be a plumber who lives in the Midwest and loves basketball. If so, at least three important life experiences mesh together to make up your one perspective. You can add another life experience to those three—religious faith—and the perspective becomes still richer, broader, differently informed, and enlightened. The point is that the "religious" is a feature in one's overall perspective, it is not the whole of one's perspective. But since it is concerned with life's ultimate meanings and values, it has a profoundly transforming influence on all the other features of a person's perspective. It becomes a "bottom line" influence in one's understanding and evaluations toward decisions for action.

We say "religious faith" in the definition rather than "Catholic" or even "Christian" faith in order to keep the exercise of theological reflection broader than it would otherwise be. What are the assumptions, beliefs, and operative dynamics of religious faith that deeply influence our understanding of issues and situations, our evaluation of them and, consequently, our choice of actions that we deem "good"? Most world religions share several beliefs in common. They are identified by Friedrich Heiler in his classic article, "The History of Religions as a Preparation for the Cooperation of Religions" (*The History of Religions*, ed. M. Eliade and J. Kitagawa, University of Chicago Press, 1959, pp. 142-153).

According to Heiler, Christianity, Judaism, Islam, Zoroastrian Mazdaism, Hinduism, Buddhism, and Taoism hold that (and please excuse the gender-exclusive language):

- There is a transcendent reality;
- He is immanent in human hearts;
- He is supreme beauty, truth, righteousness, and goodness;
- He is love, mercy, compassion;
- The way to him is repentance, self-denial, prayer;
- The way is love of one's neighbor, even of one's enemies; and
- The way is love of God, so that bliss is conceived as knowledge of God, union with him, or dissolution into him.

To these beliefs, understandings, values, or "working assumptions" of one's life perspective, Christianity adds that the transcendent reality has become a human and has forever more made human history his own with us. As "God with us" (Immanuel), he is personally present and active as a dynamic force in human persons, communities, and history. Christians believe that Jesus lives and acts in each of us in the world at large. Living in us as the Holy Spirit, Jesus guides us to recognize him acting in the world and empowers us to join him in his work of building up the Kingdom of God in our midst.

In order to do what seems best . . .

Understanding the situation or issue and evaluating the possible courses of action to remedy the situation are all geared to deciding what to do—which is essential if the remedy is to come about and be actually effective. Theological reflection culminates, that is, in action. It is not simply to gain a better understanding or appreciation (evaluation) of an issue or situation; it aims ultimately to do something about it. In that sense it is activist, even though the phases or understanding and evaluation often entail very scholarly work and theoretical analysis. The action may be setting up a soup kitchen; it may be advocating for a new or different piece of legislation; it may be opening a school or a training program. Or it may be issuing a publication and offering recommendations for others to pursue and promote. But to be complete, theological reflection needs to end up with some form of action to improve the situation.

For the improvement of our living together as a human family . . .

This is the aim and goal of the whole process of theological reflection, just as it is the aim and goal of Christ's Gospel and the Church's mission. That aim and goal of life is summed up by Jesus in the "Lord's Prayer" that he left us, "Thy Kingdom come," which is to say, "Thy will be done." It was his first sermon: "The Kingdom of God is at hand. Repent and believe the good news." Another summary is in Jesus' "Priestly Prayer" at the Last Supper, according to St. John, "That all may be one, as Thou, Father in me, and I in Thee, that they may be one in us."

Vatican II puts it this way:

God did not create the human race for life in isolation, but for the formation of social unity. So also, it has pleased God to make human beings holy and save them not merely as individuals without any mutual bonds, but by making them into a single people. . . . There everyone, as members one of the other, would render mutual service according to the different gifts bestowed on each.

For the Kingdom of justice and peace, truth and love, to flourish and reach fulfillment, many institutions and organizations must work smoothly and harmoniously together, each pursuing its particular goals, but all pursuing together the goals that are common to all of us. These common goals are required if all the members of the human family, members of Christ's body, are to participate and share equitably in the life of the family and thereby to develop their God-given potential.

* * *

Even to describe, let alone achieve, what is required economically, politically, commercially, religiously, educationally, and in the family is well beyond this short description of theological reflection. But it is not beyond the work of theological reflection. In fact, it is what theological reflection must work on—for the betterment of our human living together, and especially for our brothers and sisters who have been left out.

Adapted from a document circulated in 1995 for those taking part in Woodstock activities.

31.
A Prophetic Mission
The Martyrs of El Salvador

I'll never forget the phone call I got 15 years ago this coming Tuesday. It was about 8:00 a.m. on Thursday, November 16, 1989. And it came from a good friend at CBS television news. She said, "We just got a report from the Reuters News Service that the whole Jesuit community at the Central American University in El Salvador has been brutally killed, along with the housekeeper and her daughter."

I was stunned. I had a very vivid memory of that Jesuit community. I had lived with them when I attended the funeral of Archbishop, now Saint, Oscar Romero nine years before—in March of 1980. They were a warm and welcoming group. What I remember most were the bullet-pocked walls in the living room of their residence. There had been any number of drive-by machine gun shootings. I asked one of the Jesuits why they hadn't had the walls plastered and painted. "Two reasons," he said. "First, if we fix them today, they will probably be riddled again tomorrow. And second and more important," he said, "we want the bullet holes to be a constant reminder to us of our ministry and the price it requires of us."

Their ministry? What was that ministry? And why in the world was it worth the price of bullets and death? I've thought a lot about it and the best I can come up with is this: It was a ministry of *well-informed prophecy*. There may be a message here for us.

First, it was prophecy—a prophetic ministry and mission. A prophet is one who speaks out—with conviction and courage. And what the prophet speaks out is God's Word, as best he or she can hear and discern it in the concrete, historical events and circumstances of the here and now.

What Word of God did the Jesuits hear in their own situation in the El Salvador of the 1980s? Cesar Jerez, the Jesuit provincial in Central America at the time, described it to me this way. "There is an 'oligarchy' in El Salvador that consists of 14 wealthy families. They own most of the land in this largely agricultural country. Along with some 200 satellite families, the 14 hold most of the wealth and power in El Salvador, with *de facto*, if not *de jure*, control of the government, the paramilitary, and the police.

"Meanwhile," he explained, "the vast majority of the 4.5 million people of El Salvador struggle to survive on seasonal labor, if they are not simply unemployed. These peasants live in abject poverty, are very largely illiterate, have no voice in the political process, and experience constant threat and oppression. The oppression of the impoverished peasants and religious leaders comes from the right-wing paramilitary groups that enjoy the tolerance, if not the active support, of the government. The human rights violations are frequent and flagrant."

This was the historical situation in which Archbishop Romero and the Jesuits strove to hear the Word that God wanted them to speak out. Listen to him, as he reflects the Word he heard from God.

> The church would betray its own love for God and its fidelity to the gospel if it stopped being... a defender of the rights of the poor ... a humanizer of every legitimate struggle to achieve a more just society ... [a society] that prepares the way for the true reign of God in history.

At a later date, he said:

> When the church hears the cry of the oppressed it cannot but denounce the social structures that give rise to and perpetuate the misery from which the cry arises.

And finally, days before his murder, Archbishop Romero told a reporter:

You can tell the people that if they succeed in killing me, I forgive and bless those who do it. Hopefully, they will realize they are wasting their time. A bishop will die, but the church of God, which is the people, will never perish.

That last citation really touches me because it reminds me of the last letter I received from Archbishop Romero. It arrived on March 24, 1980. At the time I was president of the United States Conference of Jesuits and I had been working hard to help convince our government to stop sending money and equipment to the Salvadoran military and paramilitary, as Archbishop Romero and the Salvadoran Jesuits had requested of me. I had a private meeting with Secretary of State Cyrus Vance and helped arranged for the reopening of Congressional hearings on human rights violations in El Salvador. The archbishop was writing me to express his gratitude, and concluded:

Your fraternal manifestation of solidarity helps us to deepen even further our human and Christian awareness of . . . the inalienable rights of every human being in accord with the dignity of each as a person and a child of God.

That night, March 24th, I received a phone call from El Salvador telling me that the archbishop had just been shot dead while celebrating Mass. He serenely paid the price for his prophetic mission—just as the six Jesuits would, nine years later.

The prophetic mission of these Jesuits was well informed, as we have seen. This is the second characteristic of their ministry, and I will not dwell on it. It is too obvious. I will only recall that all of the Jesuit martyrs were university professors who were amazingly well published, and whose research cut deep and exercised a profound influence on their ministry of prophetic proclamation. As scholars, they joined critical intelligence to passionate commitment—mind with heart—in service to the prophetic mission of the whole Church of El Salvador.

And what of us? Is there a message here? I would suggest that, in their well-informed prophetic ministry, the Jesuit martyrs of El Salvador are issuing a call to us to "go and do likewise." As we look at our own current historical situation, what Word do we hear God uttering to us? Are we well enough informed to hear it accurately? And, if we are, have we got the prophetic courage to speak out—to act out—with the boldness of the Gospel?

Let's pray for these graces for ourselves in these ambiguous and troubled times of ours. And let's do so by calling on the intercession of the six Jesuit martyrs and the two brave women who died with them:

Ignacio Ellacuría, rector . . . **Pray for us**
Ignacio Martin-Baró, vice rector . . . **Pray for us**
Segundo Montes, professor of sociology . . . **Pray for us**
Amando López, professor of philosophy . . . **Pray for us**
Joaquin López y López, director, Center for Humanitarian Assistance . . . **Pray for us**
Juan Ramón Moreno, director of university-related programs . . . **Pray for us**
Julia Elba Ramos, dedicated collaborator, housekeeper, and cook . . . **Pray for us**
Young Celina, devoted daughter . . . **Pray for us**

From a homily at Loyola University Maryland on November 14, 2004, marking the 15ᵗʰ anniversary of the Jesuit massacre at the University of Central America.

PART IV

Leadership …

Principles and Practices for Business and Life

32.

Reflective Leadership

How to be True to "Thine Own Self"

Leadership commands both responsibilities and rewards. Many of the responsibilities are explicit, such as building revenues, maintaining profitability, and reporting to the board and other stakeholders. Other leadership mandates are implicit; notably, to lead and develop the team that will help accomplish the leader's vision and work plan at every level in the organization.

Lee Iacocca, the renowned CEO and savior of Chrysler Corporation, believed that the ability to work with and motivate a team of people was an essential management quality. "There's one phrase I hate to see on any executive's evaluation, no matter how talented he may be," he wrote in *Iacocca: An Autobiography*, published in 1984. "'He has trouble getting along with other people.' He can't get along with people? Then he's got a real problem. Because that's all we've got around here. No dogs, no apes, only people. And if he can't get along with his peers, what good is he to the company?"

Looking past his signature bluntness, Iacocca had a point. People matter in every leadership enterprise. There are probably many leadership principles and imperatives that could be culled from a general belief in people-centered management, and I've often talked about these principles with business audiences (drawing frequently from my own experiences of leadership, good and bad).

Undoubtedly one of these would be leadership's responsibility to articulate and embody the vision and mission of the organization—what we're all about. The mission needs to be clear, articulated well, recognized, embraced by participants, and constantly referenced in making new choices for the future and evaluating past performance. If we don't know *who we are* and what we are supposed to be doing, how in the world can we do it? *Gnothi seauton*, Know Thyself, was an ancient Greek aphorism, and an appropriate follow-up line is "to thine own self be true," which Polonius says to his son Laertes in Shakespeare's *Hamlet*. Another principle would have to do with the need to build and sustain a workforce of productive collaborators who are leaders in their own right. That is a further imperative for good leadership, and it calls for team building through good communications and the willingness to facilitate dialog. But for now, I'd like to focus on a leadership principle that is less-seldom articulated, one that digs more deeply into the psyche of the person who is leading. Leadership calls for:

> *Modeling and commending reliance on one's authentic self, and having the courage to follow this calling with integrity and authenticity.*

In other words, a good leader draws confidence not from the expectation of praise from others, but out of the deep faith that he or she is living with utmost authenticity. To act this way, the leader needs to know who they really are, who they are called to become, and what they are called to do.

Former Medtronic CEO Bill George talks about this in his book *True North: Discover Your Authentic Leadership*. He says, "Your True North represents who you are as a human being at your deepest level. It is your orienting point—your fixed point in a spinning world—that helps you stay on track as a leader. Your True North is based on your most cherished values, your passions and motivations, and the sources of satisfaction in your life. When you follow your True North, your leadership will be authentic, and people will naturally want to associate with you. . . . As psychologist William James wrote a century ago, 'The best way to define a person's character is to seek out the time when he felt most deeply and intensely active and alive; when he could hear his inner voice saying, 'this is the real me.'"

We could call this "True North" our *conscience*. And our conscience is our sense of responsibility to who we are in ourselves and in our relationships with other people—and, fundamentally, with God. This "voice" of "True North" is our sense of "vocation." And what we hear and feel is a calling from beyond, a calling from God—by whatever name we choose to call our Supreme Being. When we are ultimately challenged, we have an Ultimate source of affirmation and support. And this gives us the behavioral constancy that our company, our community, our government, our school, or our hospital needs for survival, growth, and a steady course into the future.

So, in summary: First, know and share your mission. Second, build and bond a collaborative team. And third, be authentic, rely on your conscience, and trust the Lord.

Another person from whom I have learned a great deal about leadership is Peter Drucker. He was a writer, professor, and management consultant, once referred to as the man who invented management. It happened this way. Jim Collins, S.J., who was on the staff of the Xavier Labor Relationship Institute in Jamshedpur, India, joined our Maryland Province staff and taught us a lot about leadership. He said it would be a good idea if the whole staff would read and discuss Peter Drucker's book, called *The Effective Executive*. And so we did.

Let me tell you some of the things I learned from Drucker—who, by the way, had great admiration for Ignatius Loyola as a leader. Though he generally kept it quiet, Drucker, like Ignatius, was also a very religious man. When his conviction that religious faith was productive of excellent business practice "slipped out," he got right to the point. Here are a couple of his observations that touch on the relevance of religious faith to business practice:

> *In this world, the ones who best understand what can make a difference are the saints. That's the definition of a saint: somebody who sees reality.*
>
> *. . . . I became interested in management because of my interest in religion and institutions. The individual needs the return to spiritual values, for he can survive in the present human situation only by reaffirming that man is not just a biological and psychological being but also a spiritual being, that is a creature, and existing for the purposes of his creator and subject to Him.*

Drucker first became interested in Ignatius Loyola for his stress on self-awareness and self-analysis. The same quality attracted him to John Calvin, the influential French theologian, pastor, and principal figure in the development of Calvinism. Management consultant and former Woodstock Theological Center fellow Terry Armstrong explains it in an article titled, "OD [Organizational Development] Practitioner, Manage Yourself." He writes:

> Success in OD comes to those who know and manage themselves. An article, *Managing Oneself*, by Peter Drucker and published in the *Harvard Business Review* sums up my feelings about the necessity of self-management. . . . He claims that "feedback analysis" was invented in the fourteenth century and picked up independently some 150 years later by John Calvin and Ignatius of Loyola. Drucker claims that Calvin and Ignatius incorporated into the practice of their followers a steadfast focus on performance and results. Practiced with religious dedication, this simple method of obtaining feedback on performance and results produced the Calvinist church and the Jesuit order. He might as well have said that it was a similar method, MBO [Management by Objectives], which built General Motors.

As reported by Jack Beatty, a senior editor at *Atlantic Monthly* and author of *The World According to Peter Drucker*, Drucker took off at least two weeks at the end of each work year to review his performance and to imagine how improvement in his service to others might be possible. In other words, he practiced what he preached: feedback analysis of performance.

The principal form of "feedback analysis" that Ignatius Loyola practiced and commended to others is called the "Examination of Consciousness." Here are the five steps, straight from The Spiritual Exercises of St. Ignatius, #34 [a fuller version and explanation of the Examen is presented in Chapter 36]:

> The first point is to give thanks to God our Lord for the favors received.

The second point is to ask for grace to know my sins and to rid myself of them.

The third point is to demand an account of my soul from the time of rising up to the present examination. I should go over one hour after another, one period after another. The thoughts should be examined first, then the words, and finally, the deeds.

The fourth point will be to ask pardon of God our Lord for my faults.

The fifth point will be to resolve to amend with the grace of God. Close with an Our Father.

Though identifying and amending sins is most prominent in the wording of this version of the Examen, it also invites us to recognize and "give thanks to God our Lord for the favors received." More to the point, the meditation offers a process of reflection upon our performance as leaders and as human beings. A later Jesuit document, Decree 26 of General Congregation 34, held in 1995, tells us to practice "feedback analysis" in the four unfolding steps of: "experience –> reflection –> decision –> action," continuously repeated.

Ignatius wants us to get FULL "feedback," which we can then submit to "analysis" and thereby lay plans, with God's grace, for future action.

... And Eight Things a Leader Does

So, what does a leader do? Let me count some of the ways.

1. A leader must embody the vision and mission of the organization, since this focus is the bond of unity and source of energy for everybody working in the organization.
2. A leader must instill the conviction in others that their basic goal together is the service they render to others, not any benefit which they derive themselves, whether it be wealth, prestige, or power in any form. In a paraphrase of John F. Kennedy, it could be put as, "Ask not what your company can do for you, but what you can do for your company."
3. A leader must cultivate leaders and leadership teams throughout

their organization and do so principally in the very doing of everyday business. In other words: with the support of occasional education/formation sessions; by insisting on self-reflection (e.g., the Ignatian Examen) and journaling; all with a view to producing and delivering quality goods or services to our public.

4. A leader must help others, first, to recognize their actual relationships within this collaborative community, secondly to appreciate what, specifically, each of those relationships calls for and requires, and third, to be willing to relate this way in smooth cooperation and collaboration so that their clients or customers are well served.

5. A leader must facilitate the process of communication, inter-communication, and dialogue. This is central for sustaining these smooth relationships and collaborative patterns among all the members of the organization. In every organization, there are actual or potential roadblocks to collaboration because individuals or groups of individuals are closed to one another or even at odds with one another. Many times these dysfunctional relationships are treated like the elephant in the living room for fear that inviting conversation would result in an outbreak of hostility and deep disruption to cooperation.

6. A good leader "sprays the house with praise" to build up in others self-confidence and their willingness to give back in gratitude for all the gifts that he/she has been given.

7. As already noted, good leaders draw confidence not from expectation of praise from others, but out of the deep faith that they are living with authenticity to themselves and who they are called to become, to be, and to do. The origin or source of this conviction is their God, however they define the supreme reality.

8. A good leader, in other words, consciously exercises servant leadership. The leader is a servant of his people and ultimately of God, as stated beautifully in the 23rd Psalm (also referred to

as "A Psalm of David").

The Lord is my shepherd; I shall not want.
  He makes me lie down in green pastures.
He leads me beside still waters.
  He restores my soul.
He leads me in paths of righteousness
  for his name's sake.

Even though I walk through the valley of the shadow of death,
  I fear no evil,
for you are with me;
  your rod and your staff,
  they comfort me.

You prepare a table before me
  in the presence of my enemies;
you anoint my head with oil;
  my cup overflows.
Surely goodness and mercy shall follow me
  all the days of my life,
and I shall dwell in the house of the Lord
  forever.

A question that I'll just leave here, for ongoing reflection . . . Who, in your experience, is a truly reflective leader?

Adapted from an unpublished manuscript shared during presentations, circa 2016.

33.
Doing Business the Jesuit Way
With the 4 M's

There is, as I've often said in talks with business people, a Jesuit way of doing business. There are organizing principles, which call us to understand the foundations of Ignatius-like behavior and learn to bring them into practice in our professional lives. I came up with the 4 M's—Mindset, Mission, Motivation, and Method—as a way to codify the avenues of influence a business person has in the company. Mindset is how we see our work and all that's around us. Mission is what we do at work. Motivation is why we work. And Method is how we do the work.

Let's look a little more closely at how each of the 4 M's function in our lives.

Mindset is the way we see things, the perspective we have of ourselves and our world. It is the "horizon" (like the skyline as we gaze out on the ocean) within which everything else, especially what we deem meaningful and valuable, is located and situated. Our mindset is our "worldview." These are all different expressions for the same thing. When someone says, "It's all in the eye of the beholder," the "eye" is the mindset, which filters what's out there as we "see" it or take it in. So, it is essentially important that our eye is clear and our mindset accurate; otherwise we are out of touch with reality. Christians pray for the "mind and heart of Christ:" to see, understand, and appreciate concrete situations the way He did and does.

Many people are completely unaware of the powerful influence that their perspective has on their lives. It takes alertness, the willingness to be self-reflective and even humble to bring it into our awareness. It influences every aspect of our behavior: how we know, how we evaluate things and people, how we make decisions, and how we act. And every step of the way, we pray (as Ignatius did) to be asking "What can I do for you?" rather than "What's in it for me?"

Motivation is what moves us, attracts us, and even impels us to action. We go for what we want, desire, find appealing, interesting, exciting, or novel, what strikes us as worthwhile, valuable, desirable, and satisfying. Such desires are feelings principally, but feelings are always about something or someone we are grasping with our senses and mind. Daniel Goleman, author of *Emotional Intelligence,* explores well how emotions or feelings are not just "mushy" stuff that trivializes and gets in the way of "real" business decisions. Just the opposite is true. Neglect to notice your feelings (i.e., the values that are really motivating you) and your decisions and you are flying blind. Our desires are legion and are also notoriously unruly. Some, if not most, very holy people spend a lifetime ignoring the urging of a base desire or two, perhaps revenge or greed. The desires we embrace and promote are major ingredients of our "Mindset." Jesus' love and desire to help the poor, the disabled, and the socially despised was so spontaneous as to be essentially "him!"

Mission is what we feel called to be and do, consistent with our Mindset and Motivation. "Mission" has a ring of breadth and duration to it. A company's mission statement lays out aspirational desires and commitments for its work force, as a promise to its customers or constituency about its behavior and service. In implementing the "Mission" there will be a variety of goals. And under goals will be a variety of strategies and tactics, according to which there will be job descriptions of the variety of collaborative responsibilities that make up the organizational design. But even bigger than a company's "Mission" can be the Mission of a lifetime for an individual or community of people like a religious community (or a charity, community association, or a private club). It is a statement of the ultimate meaning and purpose of one's life and, therefore, of life itself as understood and embraced by this person or community. This "highest level" mission commitment will flow down into and influence all the other mission statements and goals in one's life—like business mission statements, or one's expectations of marriage and family life, or one's goals in civic society, and so on.

Methodology is "the way we do things around here," consistent with the self-understanding and values of the Mindset, the desires imbedded in one's Motivation, and the sense of Mission one feels called to fulfill. In the Jesuit order we talk about "Our Way of Proceeding"—language that dates back to Ignatius himself. We also talk about a company's "M.O." or modus operandi, "way of working," and that "way" depends a lot on the company's culture (promulgated generally in the mission statement) as understood and implemented by leadership especially. There is a basic and universal structure to human performance in almost any field (family, business, government, etc.). One statement of methodology is "See, Judge, Act." The Jesuit statement is "experience, reflection, decision, and action," in a constantly cyclical and ongoing pattern.

Jesuit Bernard Lonergan spent his lifetime identifying the basic structure of human behavior by facilitating people to raise their own operations to self-awareness and asking them to describe what's "going on" in themselves. In his analysis there are four basic steps that he translated into "imperatives" (one wag calls them the "Be-Attitudes"):

Be Attentive (to what you see, hear, and so on);

Be Intelligent (by proposing an explanation(s) as to what it might actually be);

Be Reasonable (by making a judgment of fact—"It is THIS!"—on the basis of the best reasons available); and

Be Responsible (by discerning, discovering, deciding, and doing what is most valuable and helpful under the circumstances).

That's method—what Lonergan saw as a transcendental method.

* * *

By whatever name, the 4 M's are critical to living out one's vocation as a business person. All of us need to not just be able to recite but also appropriate these principles in our minds and hearts, our planning and evaluating, our hoping and dreaming—as we do business the Jesuit way.

Adapted from an unpublished manuscript on faith and business.

34.

God and the Business Person

Letter in Response to a Fortune Magazine *article*

I enclose here some reflections on the article in the July 2001 *Fortune* magazine, "God and Business." It's a good article, but for Catholic businesspersons there are some more specific questions that the article (understandably) doesn't touch.

They are questions like: How can committed Catholic businesspersons (or groups of Catholic businesspersons) best think about their responsibilities as business leaders? How does their faith form their frame of mind or viewpoint? What are the essential elements of a Catholic businessperson's vocation as distinct from Catholics in other professions?

All Catholics are called to lead lives in which their faith is integrated in both family life and work life. And all Catholics are called to fulfill their Christian vocation in both family life and the work they do, whether it is in health care, government, journalism, education, or business. But what, specifically, does the vocation of a Catholic business leader ask of him or her? What does it invite and call them to do and to become? How should they see their task and responsibility as Catholic business leaders?

What follows is not *the* answer to these questions. It is *an* answer, offered in the hope that it will stimulate reflection and discussion.

So, what's business, and what's Catholic, and what do the two have to do with one another?

A business is a group or community of people gathered together to produce and supply goods or services to others for a profit. A business leader is called to head such an enterprise as a role of service to others. And the good business leader is one who is and feels fully responsible for a company. He or she is responsible for the flourishing of the company. And to achieve this flourishing, he/she (and the whole team) has to successfully fulfill two, closely interrelated, types of goals: financial goals and non-financial goals.

The financial goals are self-evident. You've got to make a financial profit if the business is to survive and grow. The financial goal is profitability, a healthy profitability, on a long-term basis. Profits are necessary for a company to stay healthy and flourish. They are needed for growth, for reinvestment, to experiment, to provide growing opportunities to the executives and employees, and to stay competitive. Therefore, a responsible leader insists on the regular, systematic use of the accurate "yardsticks" that have been developed to measure financial performance.

How profits are used is a question each business leader or group has to decide at a given time and under the specific circumstances. It could be to invest, or to increase dividends, or to increase some benefits to executives or employees, or to lower prices to customers, or to pay more suppliers, or to experiment with new startup divisions, or the like. Decisions about how profits will be used, just like decisions about how profits are generated, will be decided by practical demands and considerations, guided by a Catholic conscience (see below). Obviously, profit is not the goal of the Catholic business leader or the business itself. Profits are necessary for the company to flourish and stay healthy.

There's no need to dwell at length on the importance of meeting financial goals. It's a constant preoccupation and worry of business people everywhere. In fact, financial goals can become such a preoccupation that it can diminish or even block advertence to other goals that are non-financial. Until recently most businesses didn't even list or evaluate non-financial goals in their annual reports. We have begun to see increased focus on "balanced scorecards" that give attention to all aspects of business performance—sales, profits, ROA [return on assets], customer satisfaction, associate satisfaction, and others.

There needs to be a lot more thinking, discussion, and development in the area of non-financial goals. Non-financial goals are all the factors, other than financial, that contribute to the flourishing of a company. Principally, they regard the many different people, all of whom need to be working together, carrying out their different functions productively and efficiently, in order for the company to be able to provide to the customer the products or services that it has chosen to focus on.

The question is how have these people flourished in and through the company. Do they form a genuine workplace community? Do they feel well respected as human beings, who are endowed by God with dignity deserving reverence? Is there care for their personal growth and development in creativity, skills, and understanding? Are they justly and generously compensated, proportionate to their contribution and the locale of employment? Are work policies "family friendly?" Is there mobility and opportunity for advancement for an industrious, dedicated, and imaginative worker? Does care for team building create and foster relationships of friendship as well as colleagueship among workers, for heightened morale and a supportive environment? In short, is the company *humane* and not simply concerned with *things*?

The fostering and development of this kind of work community needs an intelligent caring leadership that is concerned, for instance, with:

- Setting a clear direction for the company so that executives and employees can pull together to achieve a superior result;
- Having the right person in the right place;
- Developing a participative management style;
- Training people and developing their talent;
- Giving motivation, recognition, and encouragement;
- Evaluating performance;
- Cultivating honesty, helpfulness, and solidarity among all members;
- Reducing fear and encouraging freedom to speak up;
- Evaluating and creating new opportunities and tasks;
- Overseeing research that recognizes shifts in customer preferences and the underlying reasons;
- Establishing and maintaining an attractive corporate culture, in which people like to work productively, where they are helpful to each other, and where ideas and feedback are welcome;
- Setting no barriers for people to lead integrated lives, i.e., lives that can integrate faith and family with their work;
- Setting a standard by the leader's own commitment and behavior.

Why should Catholic business leaders pay attention to these non-financial goals? Is it because by doing so they will achieve long-term profitability which is the only goal that counts in the financial market? For the Catholic businessperson, the answer has to be an emphatic "no." Members of the work community are not and never can be means to an end (in this case, profit). Humans are ends in themselves. Pope John Paul II loves to say, "Human beings are the only creatures under the sun that can never be ends for another purpose." They have an inviolable and intrinsic dignity, which is God given.

In the eyes of a Catholic business leader, therefore, people have to be given the chance to grow as human beings. They should have the opportunities to achieve the same goal that the Catholic business leader is called to by God: a fully integrated human life (faith, family, and work life).

We see here how our Catholic faith shapes our frame of mind and perspective. It helps us see each person as created in the image and likeness of God, so that he and she deserve our utmost respect. Our instruction and inspiration come from the life and teaching of Jesus Christ. What we learn from seeing him in action and listening to his teaching is:

- We all have one Father.
- We are here to do his will.
- We are to serve others.
- We are co-creators with God, creating wealth and opportunities.
- We are instruments in his hands as we do our work.
- We should lead integrated lives.
- We should be listening to his Spirit in us.
- We should see with his eyes and feel with his heart.
- We should be full of thanks and praise.
- We should enjoy the beauty of his creation and be inspired to keep it in its splendor.
- We should enjoy and spread joy.
- We should live in Him as He lives in us.
- Our work should be our prayer.
- Our prayer should inform our work.

Therefore, the leader serves the needs of the company and the work community, and by working well together, the members of this community are able to serve their customers.

That is the principal vocation of a Catholic business leader. In addition, a business leader should also be interested in larger social concerns and opportunities, even though he lacks direct control over or particular expertise in these matters. Other professions have a direct responsibility for certain of these matters—health care, education, human rights, ecology, and government agencies involved in setting interest rates, devising import restrictions, revising tax levels, watching over unemployment rates and the consumer confidence index, and so on. In all these different areas, Catholic professionals should pool their expertise and resources to promote and care for the common good of all. It is part of our human responsibility, especially for those of us who have been privileged with education and material means.

But such service should never detract from the business leader's primary responsibility for the flourishing of the company—for both its financial stability and the wellbeing of the workforce and its community. If this is the primary responsibility of business leaders, then they exercise their best influence by articulating, measuring, and registering the performance and progress of both kinds of goals for the company—financial and non-financial.

Excerpted from an unpublished letter/essay dated November 22, 2002, signed by Father Jim Connor and written in conversation with Catholic business leader and philanthropist Anthony Brenninkmeyer.

35.

Discernment of Spirits

Making Decisions, the Ignatian Way

Leadership is intertwined with mission, which enables us to lead—and to decide. In particular, our mission enables what I call the Ignatian "3 D's"—discernment (or deliberation), decision making, and doing. Here I'll put the accent on how to decide the Ignatian way, but first, I'll say a few words about Christ's mission.

Jesus described his mission in his opening proclamation, which describes his entire life's commitment: The Kingdom of God is at hand. Repent! Have a change of mind and heart, and believe that this is really Good News! The exact text in Mark's Gospel (1:12-15) is this:

> The Spirit drove Jesus out into the wilderness. He was in the wilderness for forty days, tempted by Satan and he was with the wild beasts. . . . Then after John the Baptist was arrested, Jesus came to Galilee, proclaiming the good news of God, and saying, "Now is the time. The Kingdom of God is at hand. Repent, and believe in the good news."

Over time, people began to realize that "the Kingdom of God" was the whole human family in which all of us are living together as loving and caring brothers and sisters. The preface of the Mass of Christ the King describes the Kingdom of God as us people living together in "truth and life, holiness and grace, justice, love, and peace." And this is the first petition of the "Our Father," the prayer which Jesus taught his apostles to pray. "Our Father . . . Thy Kingdom come . . . on earth as it is in heaven."

Our mission is to collaborate with Christ in his mission of bringing the Kingdom of God to realization on earth. To collaborate with

Christ in bringing the Kingdom of God to fulfillment on earth is an exercise of LOVE—God's love for us, our love for God, and our love for one another. Ignatius describes it in the final meditation of his Spiritual Exercises. It is called, "A Contemplation to Attain Love." Here are two key sections in that meditation (#'s 235-236):

I will consider how God dwells in creatures; in the elements, giving them existence; in the plants, giving them life; in the animals, giving them sensation; in human beings, giving them intelligence; and finally, how in this way he dwells also in myself, giving me existence, life, sensation, and intelligence; and even further, making me his temple, since I am created as a likeness and image of the Divine Majesty.

I will consider how God labors and works for me in all the creatures on the face of the earth; that is, he acts in the manner of one who is laboring. For example, he is working in the heavens, elements, plants, fruits, cattle, and all the rest—giving them their existence, conserving them, concurring with their vegetative and sensitive activities, and so forth.

God's dwelling in and laboring for each and everything and every person is an expression of his LOVE. Ours is a God who labors in love—love of us and for us!

We come to understand how to co-labor with God by DISCERNING his active presence in our history here and now, and then DECIDING how we are being invited to join him and to COLLABORATE with him.

The very first thing we want to discern, of course, is whether, in this effort, we are being "inspired" by the Holy Spirit or by the Evil Spirit, namely, Satan. For instance, who or what is "moving" me to volunteer for a demanding service in an inner-city community? Or, who or what is "inspiring" me to write a check in the amount of five hundred thousand dollars to donate to the Red Cross? Am I on an "ego-trip" or am I really moved by genuine compassion for others?

Ignatius lays out these polar-opposite alternatives in a meditation in the Spiritual Exercises called the "Two Standards" in which "Standards" means flags or banners under which people are invited to march. One is

Satan's "standard" and the other is Christ's. On Satan's "standard" we read that possessions lead to prestige, and then to pride (an "ego-trip"). On Christ's "standard" we read: Simplicity of lifestyle leads to willingness for humiliation, which in turn leads to loving service of others. In shorthand, I describe Satan's standard as "What's in it for me?" Whereas Christ's standard is "What can I do for you?"

In the Spiritual Exercises (#'s 169-182), Ignatius lays out three ways in which we can do a discernment and make good decisions.

In making a good decision I ought to focus only on the purpose for which I am created, i.e., to love and praise God our Lord and to serve my human brothers and sisters. Accordingly, whatever I decide ought to be chosen as an aid toward that end.

The First Way of making a decision happens when God our Lord so moves and attracts the will that a sincere and good person, without doubting or being able to doubt, chooses and does what was proposed. This is what St. Paul and St. Matthew did when they followed Christ's call to them, "Follow me!" They dropped everything and followed immediately.

The Second Way happens when a good person is drawn to reach understanding and make a decision in light of their experience of "consolation" and "desolation"—peace and joy or deep disturbance—at the prospect of choosing one or another option. From the experience of feelings of consolations and desolations, one can discern God's will and decide accordingly.

The Third Way is to list over time the advantages and disadvantages of option A and option B for praising God and serving one's neighbor. When the two lists are complete, the person carefully considers, ponders, and weighs the alternate advantages and disadvantages and allows their mind and heart to be drawn toward the choice that is more favorably commended.

In all three of these ways, the decision is subsequently held up to God for testing and confirmation. And a prayer of gratitude is offered.

In "The Second Way," Ignatius speaks of "consolation" and "desolation." (We experience the effects of consolation and desolation differently, depending on whether, at that particular time, we are living more in keeping with the standard or Christ, or of Satan.) Elsewhere in the Exercises (#'s 315-316) he describes what he means by those words:

It is characteristic of the evil spirit [desolation] to harass with anxiety, to conflict with sadness, to raise obstacles backed by fallacious reasonings that disturb the soul. Thus he seeks to prevent the soul from advancing.

It is characteristic of the good spirit [consolation], however, to give courage and strength, consolations, inspirations, and peace. This he does by making all easy, by removing all obstacles so that the soul goes forward in doing good.

Then, Ignatius tells us to ask ourselves some very practical "questions" about our disposition in making a discernment, or decision:

1. "On my death bed would I be pleased to have made this decision this way?" (Spiritual Exercises # 186)
2. "Would this have been my advice to a fellow human being?" (Spiritual Exercises #185)
3. "Would I have wanted to have decided this way as I stand before my Lord and Savior on judgment day?" (Spiritual Exercises #187)

Finally, this process of discernment leading to decision and action is beautifully described in Decree 26 of the 34th Jesuit General Congregation:

The God of Ignatius is the God who is at work in all things: laboring for the salvation of all.

For a Jesuit, therefore, not just any response to the needs of the men and women of today will do. The initiative must come from the Lord laboring in events and people here and now. God invites us to join with him in his labors, on his terms, and in his way. To discover and join the Lord, laboring to bring everything to its fullness, is central to the Jesuit way of proceeding. It is the Ignatian method of prayerful discernment, which can be described as a constant interplay between experience, reflection, decision, and action, in line with the Jesuit ideal of being [a] contemplative in action. Through individual and communal apostolic discernment, lived in obedience, Jesuits take responsibility for their apostolic choices in today's world. Such discernment reaches out, at the same time, to embrace the larger community of all those with whom we labor in mission.

Notice the firm belief that God is present and laboring within our personal and unfolding history as we saw in the "Contemplation to Attain Love." We discern in order to discover God present here and now so we can decide how we can and should collaborate with him in his mission of building the Kingdom of God on earth—of gathering us all together as loving brothers and sisters in God's own family. God's mission, fundamentally, is making us blessed, fulfilled, and delighted. As Jesus said, "I come not to be served but to serve, and to give my life for others—all others" (Mark 10:45).

Adapted from source material for various talks.

36.

Practicing the Ignatian Examen

Five Steps for Daily Discernment and Inspired Leadership

The only form of prayer Jesuits must do daily is "The Examination of Consciousness," typically referred to as "The Examen." Ignatius said that, given our crowded schedules and unexpected demands on our time, we may not be able to make a meditation or even attend or offer Mass, and that's fine. We have to put first things first. But the ONE thing we must NEVER omit is the Examen. The Examen is an Ignatian discernment—in short form—of how God has been leading us, or at least TRYING to lead us, in the course of this day, and how well we responded.

Here are some presuppositions in doing the Examen:

1. God's creating is a continual sharing of Trinitarian life with all creation, praying that God's Kingdom come on earth as in heaven, i.e., "that all may be one, as Thou, Father in me, and I in Thee, that they may be one in us" (John 17:21).
2. Thus present in creation and within human history, God is actively guiding us toward the full attainment of this life with God and one another in unity and peace, justice and love, in quite concrete ways.
3. We humans can, with God's grace, discern the direction of God's active guidance to this end in our own daily history, and we can collaborate with God to promote the Kingdom's realization in society.
4. The sign of God's guidance is what produces unity and peace among people and what instills feelings of peace, love, and

integrity in us. By contrast, what produces dissension and hostility in society and selfishness and revenge in us is a sign of the destructive activity of evil (see Galatians 5:13-26).

And here is one traditional version of the steps in making the Ignatian Examen:

1. We begin by quieting ourselves. Ask to be made aware of God's goodness in the many gifts of life and love. Be thankful.
2. Pray for the grace to see clearly, to understand accurately, and to respond generously to the guidance God is giving us in our daily history.
3. Review in memory the history of the day (week, month, etc.) in order to be shown concrete instances of the presence and guidance of God and, perhaps, of the activity and influence of evil. These can be detected by paying attention to strong feelings we experienced either at the time or now as we review these incidents or encounters.
4. Evaluate how we behaved in these instances: whether we collaborated with God or yielded to the influence of evil in some way. Pray to feel and express gratitude and regret appropriate to the circumstances.
5. Ask to be shown how to collaborate more effectively with God and how, with God's assistance, to avoid or overcome the influence of evil in the future. Resolve and decide.

Conclude with an "Our Father."

* * *

There's a short-hand way of capturing the unfolding steps in the Examen. Three simple questions:

"What happened?" This question is asking for facts, gathering the data of experience.

"So what?" Here, we ask for the meaning of the data, including our motivation, so we could interpret and understand them, and finally say, "This is what is!"

"Now what?" We ask what, if anything, we are going to do about it. It's an action question.

In the Jesuit cycle, this is experience, reflection, decision, and action in a spiraling and ongoing way. We recall what happened, reflect on its meaning, and after imagining various options, we decide on our future behavior and then do it. These are the classic 3 D's: deliberate, decide, and do.

37.

Homily for a Leader

Memorial Liturgy for Pedro Arrupe

We are gathered this evening to remember and to be grateful for one of God's most precious gifts to the Society of Jesus and the Church: Pedro Arrupe. I propose we refresh our memories, so that we can give fitting thanks.

I will first recall the highlights of Father Arrupe's life, and then share some personal reminiscences, in the hope that they will evoke some of your own.

First, then, the highlights of his life.

He was born on November 14, 1907, in Bilbao, Spain. (He was the first Basque to hold the office of Jesuit Superior General since St. Ignatius. He used to joke, "One Basque founded the Society and another one is destroying it!")

He pursued medical studies with distinction at the University of Madrid from 1922 to 1927, when he decided to enter the Society of Jesus.

His study of philosophy in Belgium and of theology in Holland and the United States equipped him with three of the languages in which he would become fluent. There were seven altogether: Japanese, English, French, Italian, German, Latin, and Spanish.

He was ordained to the priesthood in 1936, and, after a brief stay in Mexico, went to Japan where he would spend the next 30 years. He worked in pastoral ministry, before becoming director of novices and then Provincial Superior. It was in 1945, as novice-master in a residence on the outskirts of Hiroshima, that he was the first one to provide medical assistance to the victims of the atom bomb.

In May, 1965, at the 31st General Congregation of the Society of Jesus, Father Arrupe was elected Superior General.

In 1980, after confidential consultation with his own counsellors and with all the Provincials in the world, he requested the Holy See to approve the calling of a General Congregation to accept his resignation as General for reasons of age and health—and to elect his successor. The Holy See did not grant this request (more on that in a moment).

A year later, in 1981, Father Arrupe suffered the stroke which would debilitate him for the rest of his life. The Holy Father appointed Father Paul Dezza as his personal delegate to govern the Society until 1983. For ten years, Father Arrupe lived in the infirmary in the Jesuit headquarters until his death on February 5, 1991.

I would like now to share some personal reminiscences which capture three special qualities of Father Arrupe: his trust; his personal style of governance; and his service under the Cross of Christ.

The story of my first meeting with him is a perfect example of his trust. He had appointed me provincial superior of the Maryland Province, sight unseen, in August of 1968. It is important for the story to recall the circumstances of those days—rather stormy days, we might say. Martin Luther King and Bobby Kennedy had just been assassinated the spring before, and racial tensions were running high. The pope's encyclical on birth control, *Humanae vitae*, had just come out in July. The Vietnam War was at its height, and antiwar sentiment was rife. The Catonsville Nine, led by Jesuit Dan Berrigan, were about to go on trial in Baltimore. Vatican II's "winds of change" were sweeping through the church. And on all these issues Jesuits were split.

This was the context within which I got a cable from the Superior General's office my first week in office. It said, "Come to Rome immediately." I cabled back that, perhaps, it would be a good idea for me to go in a month or so, after I had a chance to learn something about the job of provincial. His office cabled back, and a representative told me, "Come immediately." I went.

[As related similarly in Section 1 of this book:]

With trepidation I tapped on his office door the day after I arrived in Rome. He opened it personally, greeted me warmly, and stood with me in the doorway. He said, *Before we sit down, there is one thing I want*

you to know. And if there is nothing else you learn from this weeklong visit,
it will have been well worth all the time and money. It is this: I trust you.
In this day and age, with things moving as quickly as they are, there will be
times when you will have to make a decision that, according to the book, the
General should be consulted about first. If you feel you need to decide it, go
ahead and do so, and I will support you. And if, at any time, you begin to
feel that I am not supporting you or showing confidence in you, I want you to
pick up the telephone immediately and call me—reverse the charges—so we
can get it straight immediately. If there is one thing we cannot tolerate in the
Society these days, it is a lack of trust.

I have spent a great deal of time on this story because I think it typifies so much of the greatness of Pedro Arrupe. He was able to trust his fellow Jesuits, not only because of his own self-confidence, but especially because of his faith in God. He was absolutely convinced that God was working in others and in the rapid changes of those days. And so he was always open to look and search for God in the signs of the times. He had an infectious, constructive confidence, as he moved us into the future. And it gave us the freedom to share in this initiative.

Another dimension of his trust in God and others—and this is my second point—was the wonderfully personal style of his governance. Throughout the 1960s many of the traditional structures of the Society of Jesus were fading away. Things like the prescribed order of the day, the dress code, custom books, and so on. Some feared we would lose all sense of unity and identity.

But it was the genius and special gift of Father Arrupe to create a Jesuit community rooted in responsible, personal relationships, in place of the organization regulated by rules. He made it his mission to get to know as many Jesuits as possible, person to person and face to face. He came to know thousands of Jesuits by first name. And he encouraged Jesuits to get to know one another, mixing us up in meetings of all kinds, thereby building up the Society as a genuinely international body. He gathered new provincials together as an international group every year for an orientation process at [the retreat facility] Villa Cavaletti. And every two years he would hear the "Manifestation of Conscience" of every provincial. He circled the globe four times and made numerous other trips to get to know Jesuits and their works personally.

And it was always a tonic for him and for us to have him visit. He was energized by visiting people: he would start a trip tired and come home refreshed. And his warmth, imagination, enthusiasm, and charismatic vision were invariably a source of inspiration and hope for others. He loved a good time: swapping jokes, telling stories, and kidding others. That is one reason he loved to have [his Vicar General] Father Vinnie O'Keefe around him. He had a trained singing voice, and would regale us with operatic arias at the least instigation. He loved life and the Society. In himself he made the Society a living, vibrant community of men.

Of course, he drove more than one management consultant crazy. He instinctively resisted organization, bureaucracy, and formal business procedures. He governed, rather, by intuition and informal consultation. He would get an idea and take it to every group he chanced upon, trying it out for reactions. His life was one long group discernment process, a process that built trust and community, as apostolic directions for the Society's future emerged and were clarified.

This brief profile would not be complete without mentioning, in the third place, that he was clearly a man of the Cross of Christ. If anyone lived and labored *Sub Vexillo Crucis*, Under the Standard of the Cross, it was Pedro Arrupe. He put enormous demands on himself, physical, spiritual, and personal. He slept an average of four hours a night, going to bed about midnight and rising about 4 or 4:30 a.m. for an hour's prayer before a quick breakfast and work. His correspondence was voluminous, he gave thousands of talks, many of which are published, and all of this on top of the ordinary governance of the Society. He was slight of build, held together—we always thought—by rawhide and bailing wire. Another secret to his stamina was his marvelous gift for catnapping. He could go out like a light for five minutes, any time or any place, no matter how intense the schedule or tense the next meeting.

In all of this driving activity his major concern was for the poor and socially deprived. He will be remembered as the Jesuit General with a heart for social justice. I dare to say that without him there never would have been "Our Mission Today," the decree of [the 1974-1975] General Congregation 32, which set the Jesuit apostolic agenda for our time. By word and example, he had laid the foundation and spirit for that mission mandate.

And, before we voted on that decree, he gave the members of the congregation a very somber speech. "Think carefully," he said, "about what you are proposing to do. Pass this decree, and you will be inviting great suffering for the Society, perhaps bloodshed. To pursue justice in the service of our faith is a very costly enterprise. Are you ready for that?" Then, he gave us a day of prayer before voting. It is easy now in retrospect to see how right he was.

His own suffering was anguish and distress when the Holy Father refused his request to call a General Congregation in order to receive his resignation as General and elect a replacement. That period was an uncertain limbo for him and the whole Society. He knew he was the object of suspicion, if not disapproval. This hurt him deeply. He was a lame duck—unable to move ahead, much less go backward.

He confided this to me one day, as I talked with him alone in his office in 1981. To cheer him up I asked him if he had ever read Milton's poem about his blindness, with the famous last line, "He also serves who only stands and waits." He perked right up. "That's wonderful," he said, "I must get that down," and he ran right over to his battered, old portable typewriter and tapped out the lines. Not long after that, he suffered his stroke, and Milton's line became ever the more fitting. As he lay in bed for the better part of ten years, he had ample time to reflect … *He also serves who only stands—or sits, or lies—and waits.* When I visited him a little over a year ago, I thought, what a strange will God has for such a dynamic, nomadic, charismatic little man!

This was his final crucifixion with Christ crucified. As he gave us an example of vitality throughout his Generalate, he also gave us an example of long-suffering patience at the end. And having died with Christ in life, he now rejoices with Him in glory forever.

Amen.

Homily delivered at a memorial liturgy for Pedro Arrupe on February 8, 1991.

Afterword

A Toast by Walter Burghardt

Our God is nothing if not ceaseless surprise. At times delightfully surprising.

At crucial crossroads in the lives of Loyola College hopefuls, God sent them an enthusiastic theology professor, and he proceeded to make human sense out of original sin—their own and his.

At a significant stage in the story of the Maryland Jesuits, God anointed an energetic young priest as provincial, and he transformed the province with a set of powerful addresses, a fresh vision of the faith that inflames.

At a troublesome time in the life of all American Jesuits, God gave us a National Conference president who could speak with imagination and passion to young and old from rock-ribbed Maine to quake-shaken California.

At a high point in the hallowed history of Holy Trinity, God laid hands on a pastor who not only shepherded with a gentle staff but, against all odds, could move little children to listen wide-eyed and openmouthed to a homily at their first Holy Communion.

At a critical moment in the life of the Woodstock Theological Center, God surprised us with a director who moved our social apostolate to parish justice, to the business world, to Latin America, even seduced the fellows into a continual intellectual sweat over a tough-minded theologian named Bernard Lonergan, encouraged a resurrection of John Courtney Murray, and delighted to sponsor three fascinating volumes unveiling not only the American hierarchy but the throne of Peter himself.

Not quite satisfied, our imaginative God sent a sexagenarian to the Jesuits' General Congregation in Rome, to make sure that 24,000 of us would express public contrition for our part in the second-class citizenship of women and ensure that our faith would be not lifeless but a faith that does justice—justice especially to those who share more of Jesus' crucifixion than of his resurrection.

Most surprising of all, the God of surprises packaged all of these surprises into one person. And so this blessed evening we lift our glasses high, lift our hearts even higher, in tribute to James L. Connor, professor, provincial, president, pastor, and priest. But best of all, to a Companion of Jesus, for fifty years rich with grace from God and grace to us: the grace of a friendship that has quietly, softly persuaded each of us to be better than we were likely to be.

For these years, for these blessings, for your friendship, Jim, we bless you and thank you. With a Gaelic wind of the Spirit behind you, would you kindly gift us with as close to 50 more years as your aching back can stand?

Shalom!

Father Walter Burghardt, S.J., (1914-2008) served as editor in chief of Theological Studies *for 23 years, before becoming a senior fellow at the Woodstock Theological Center. This selection is taken from his toast to honor Father Connor, on 50 years a Jesuit.*

Acknowledgments and Gratitude

First and foremost, I am very grateful to my family, who urged me to tell my story in writing. Special thanks to my cousins, Brian and Helen Heekin, whose encouragement, trust, and confidence gave new energy to the project as it expanded from an autobiography to include a collection of homilies and other writings as well.

Words cannot express my gratitude to Beth Kostelac and Bill Bole for their hard work and their determination to bring all of this material together to share with others. Beth started working with me on the manuscript in November of 2017 and Bill answered our clarion call for help in the fall of 2018. We co-labored *Ad Majorem Dei Gloriam.*

We share deep appreciation to Holy Trinity parishioners, Woodstock Theological Center friends, Loyola University colleagues, and others who encouraged us along the way. Gratitude especially to John and Peggy Douglas for their friendship, loyalty, and moral support all through the process.

We are grateful to Nita Crowley, who read the first draft of the manuscript and penned the foreword. Her words inspired and energized us as we continued our work.

To Dolores Leckey, who read the manuscript and gave us her critique and thoughtful reflections, we are deeply indebted. Her hospitality, warmth, and advice sustained us through to completion. We also want to thank the staff of the Institute for Advanced Jesuit Studies at Boston College, for their timely advice as we checked a number of historical details.

Finally, we are most grateful to Tim Brown, my Jesuit brother and former provincial, who believed strongly in the project and connected us to Apprentice House Press at Loyola University Maryland. Warm thanks, along that line, to Apprentice House's director, Kevin Atticks, who shepherded the manuscript through the production process and into print.

Apprentice House Press

Loyola University Maryland

Apprentice House is the country's only campus-based, student-staffed book publishing company. Directed by professors and industry professionals, it is a nonprofit activity of the Communication Department at Loyola University Maryland.

Using state-of-the-art technology and an experiential learning model of education, Apprentice House publishes books in untraditional ways. This dual responsibility as publishers and educators creates an unprecedented collaborative environment among faculty and students, while teaching tomorrow's editors, designers, and marketers.

Outside of class, progress on book projects is carried forth by the AH Book Publishing Club, a co-curricular campus organization supported by Loyola University Maryland's Office of Student Activities.

Eclectic and provocative, Apprentice House titles intend to entertain as well as spark dialogue on a variety of topics. Financial contributions to sustain the press's work are welcomed. Contributions are tax deductible to the fullest extent allowed by the IRS.

To learn more about Apprentice House books or to obtain submission guidelines, please visit www.apprenticehouse.com.

Apprentice House Press
Communication Department
Loyola University Maryland
4501 N. Charles Street
Baltimore, MD 21210
Ph: 410-617-5265
info@apprenticehouse.com
www.apprenticehouse.com